2 KINGS

BERIT OLAM
Studies in Hebrew Narrative & Poetry

2 Kings

Robert L. Cohn

David W. Cotter, O.S.B.
Editor

Jerome T. Walsh
Chris Franke
Associate Editors

A Michael Glazier Book
THE LITURGICAL PRESS
Collegeville, Minnesota

A Michael Glazier Book published by The Liturgical Press

Cover design by Ann Blattner

1   2   3   4   5   6   7   8

Library of Congress Cataloging-in-Publication Data

Cohn, Robert L.
    2 Kings / Robert L. Cohn ; David W. Cotter, editor ; Jerome T. Walsh, Chris Franke, associate editors.
        p.   cm.
    Includes bibliographical references and index.
    ISBN 0-8146-5054-6 (alk. paper)
    1. Bible. O.T. Kings, 2nd—Commentaries.   I. Title: Second Kings.
II. Cotter, David W.   III. Walsh, Jerome T., 1942– .   IV. Franke, Chris.
V. Title.

BS1335.3.C65   1999
22'.5407—dc21   99-049660
                                                          CIP

For
Gideon,
Michael,
and Jonathan
Isaiah 54:13

CONTENTS

INTRODUCTION

The Second Book of Kings is a direct continuation of 1 Kings and is incomprehensible without it. The parade of the kings of Israel and Judah, begun in 1 Kings, is completed in 2 Kings as the histories of those kingdoms march toward their respective ends. As well, prophecies launched in 1 Kings are fulfilled in 2 Kings, and the stories of particular personalities, notably Elijah, are brought to a conclusion. The rather arbitrary break between the two books must not be allowed to obscure the continuity of their content.[1]

At the same time, 2 Kings is not only a continuation. Most of what happens in the book is unanticipated by the reader even if its writers knew where they were heading all along. Despite the sometimes heavy hand of prophecy pointing toward a destiny decreed from on high, the narrative manages to surprise and provoke as it wends its way through the lives of kings and prophets. Moreover, the material with which the book deals clearly presented a set of challenges to the writers which were different from those that faced the writers of 1 Kings. Before offering a preview of those challenges, however, I must comment briefly on the general aim of this commentary.

With the use of words such as "narrative," "reader," and "writers," I have already signaled the literary thrust of this commentary. Although the intention of 2 Kings would appear to be historical, offering as it does a primarily chronological account of the reigns of real kings in real time, the book itself is a literary creation. The historical information that lies behind 2 Kings has been subordinated to a narrative concerned

---

[1] In the rabbinic tradition the two books are counted as a single book, and the division between them first appears in some medieval manuscripts and, in print, in the Bamberg edition of 1516–1517. See Steven Holloway, "Kings, Book of 1–2," *The Anchor Bible Dictionary* Vol. IV (New York: Doubleday, 1992) 69–70.

with the meaning of the events that it describes. Even if the purpose of
the book is to witness to what its authors believed to be historical reality, their representation of that reality in narrative form is, by definition,
literary. The very selection, arrangement and highlighting of material
and the employment of literary conventions in creative fashion bear
witness to the literary dimension of history writing. The purpose of this
commentary, then, is to lay bear some of that literary dimension. What
such an examination entails is explained by Jerome T. Walsh in exem-
plary fashion in his Introduction to *1 Kings* in this Berit Olam series.[2] I
can do no better than to refer you to his explanation there of central literary categories: structural issues; verbal techniques; narrative, narrator and author; plot and point of view; and characterization. All of these
categories recur here in my commentary on 2 Kings.

A literary perspective, let me be clear, in no way vitiates the importance of historical criticism, for more than a century the main approach
to 2 Kings. Historical critics have sought to identify the multiple sources
that lie behind the biblical text as we have it, and some have hypothe-
sized pre-exilic and exilic editions of the entire work. Even the biblical
narrators themselves acknowledge dependence upon earlier docu-
ments in the formulaic repetition made part of the account of each king:
"The rest of the acts of King So-and-so, which he did, are they not written in the book of acts of the kings of Israel (or Judah)?" (e.g., 2 Kgs.
1:18; 8:23, etc.). While I take as a given the manifestly composite nature
of 2 Kings, and have relied on the historical scholarship that has eluci-
dated it, the approach here is a different one. The aim of a literary commentary is not the sources, but the discourse, not the genesis of the text,
but "the text itself as a pattern of meaning and effect."[3]

That is, while historical scholarship has revealed seams in the narrative that betray antecedent written or oral texts, I present a continuous reading of the narrative that tries to appreciate the literary choices
made in its composition. Why does the text say this rather than that?
What is summarized and what is spelled out in detail? Why is this in
narration and that in dialogue? When does a character speak and
when is he or she silent? Why is the standard word order changed here
or the chronological order interrupted there? What are we told, and
what are we not told? When does the narrator offer judgments and
when do events speak for themselves? When and why does the point
of view in a narrative shift? How does the literary structure of a narra-

---

[2] Jerome T. Walsh, *1 Kings,* Berit Olam: Studies in Hebrew Narrative and Poetry
(Collegeville: The Liturgical Press, 1996) xii–xxi.

[3] Meir Sternberg, *The Poetics of Biblical Narrative: Ideological Literature and the Drama
of Reading* (Bloomington: Indiana University Press, 1985) 15.

tive bear on its meaning? How does this episode relate to those that surround it? When we begin to hypothesize other ways in which a writer could have told a story, we get a better grip on the meaning and effect of his or her chosen way of telling. By paying close attention to the way in which a writer has constructed a narrative world, we can see more clearly its historical, ideological, and esthetic dimensions.

In the case of the book of 2 Kings, as I suggested above, the writers faced unique problems in their efforts to construct a coherent history and theology. Even the casual reader is struck, first of all, by the narrative's effort to coordinate the histories of Israel in the north and Judah in the south. Rather than chronicle one history first and then go back and chronicle the other, the narrative shuttles back and forth between the two kingdoms, finishing the reign of a king in one kingdom and doubling back to pick up the story of his contemporary in the other. But if an especially lengthy reign in one extends over that of several in the other, the narrative stays in the second kingdom to complete those reigns before returning to the first.

As a biblical mode of representing simultaneity, this pattern of alternation is not unique. Think, for instance, of the switching between Joseph in Egypt to Jacob in Canaan (Gen 41:47–47:12), or of the shifting back and forth between the camps of David and Absalom as they prepare for battle (2 Samuel 15–17). But in Kings the scope and scale of the pattern produce what Meir Sternberg, in a characteristically seminal article, calls "Kings-size alternation."[4] He compares alternation with juxtaposition (which here would mean separate histories of North and South) as strategies for indicating simultaneity and argues that alternation makes for unity and interaction between the two narrative lines. I would add that by linking the stories of North and South together through alternation, the writer subordinates the contrasts between the kingdoms—dynastic instability vs. stability, Jeroboam as negative paradigm vs. David as positive paradigm, apostasy vs. loyalty to God, for example—to overriding commonalities: the appeal to divine mercy, the divine control over history, and the covenant binding both Israel and Judah to God. Now the interlocking, alternating pattern of regnal accounts is not a straitjacket demanding equal time or treatment for all reigns nor binding the writer to draw one story to a hasty conclusion in order to pick up the ball in the other kingdom. On the contrary, the arrangement, while providing a context of orderliness

---

[4] "Time and Space in Biblical (Hi)story Telling: The Grand Chronology," *The Book and the Text: The Bible and Literary Theory,* ed. Regina Schwartz (Cambridge, MA: Blackwell, 1990) 111.

and evenhandedness, permits great flexibility to run ahead or double back in time and to emphasize the affairs in one kingdom over those in the other. Along the way in the commentary, I will have occasion to illustrate this flexibility.

As if the intertwining of the history of the two kingdoms were not enough of an organizational challenge, another scheme of historical ordering competes with it in 2 Kings. This is the pattern of prophecy and fulfillment that overarches, intersects, and sometimes subverts the regnal ordering. Like missiles, a series of prophecies, sometimes by named, sometimes by anonymous prophets, and even by the divine voice itself, are launched into the history of the kingdoms to find their targets at future moments. The longest range prophecy is the *vaticinium post eventum* naming of King Josiah by the man of God from Judah (1 Kgs 13:2), not fulfilled until 2 Kgs 23:16-18.[5] But under the high trajectory of this prophecy a number of others span the reigns of the kings, bringing the whole history under repeated and overlapping divine judgments.

While divine control is implicit in the regnal pattern, exuded by its very formulaic nature, it is explicit in the prophetic words that are shot like arrows into time, bringing about events by their very enunciation. Prophetic oracles disturb the orderly sequence of regnal formulas, roil the royal history. They drop like land mines into the present, certain to be tripped by future happenings. They serve too as a reminder that history is not simply the unrolling of the careers of kings and dynasties, but is impinged upon dramatically by divine reaction to human freedom, by divine snit over royal writ. Yet prophecy, for its part, does not point to the future unambiguously. The writer of the book(s) of Kings, at least, plays fast and loose with prophecy, using its fulfillment creatively, sacrificing historical literalism for theological message. Here too the commentary provides illustrative examples.

A third challenge faced by the writer of 2 Kings was the incorporation of the many tales about the prophet Elisha and the transformation of them into a unique example of biblical hagiography. While other prophets appear in 1–2 Kings, only Elisha is accorded sustained attention. In a series of episodes, some short and others quite complex, the character of a charismatic wonder worker emerges. Introduced in 1 Kings 19 as Elijah's successor, he comes into his own in 2 Kings 2 upon Elijah's death when he inherits a "double portion" of the elder prophet's spirit (vv. 9, 15). Tales of his miracles, only loosely related to the royal history

---

[5] Biblical scholars generally understand the naming of King Josiah by a prophet who would have lived about 300 years earlier to be an example of a prophecy written after the event which it prophesies occurred.

of Israel, define the first part of 2 Kings (1:1-8:6). But after Elisha is memorialized and his great deeds recounted as if he were dead (8:1-6), he enters the narrative again, this time to challenge the political order directly by triggering revolutions in Aram, Israel, and, by extension, Judah. His fleeting appearances frame what I have defined as the second part of 2 Kings (8:7-13:25). The variety of traditions about Elisha thus contribute to a multi-faceted portrait of a prophet playing a critical role in the lives of common people and in the destiny of the nations.

Having just referred to the first two parts of 2 Kings, let me remark on the structure of the book as a whole. Structure, as I understand it here, is not inscribed in the book in an objective way, but is a matter of interpretation. To perceive structure—order, balance, symmetry, repetition—in a work is an important aspect of understanding its meaning. It follows, then, that different readers may see the structure of the same work differently. I find a four-part structure in 2 Kings. Part One (1:1-8:6), as I have said, focuses on the miracles of Elisha. It begins with the last of Elijah's confrontations (1:2-18) and the tale of his miraculous ascent and Elisha's succession (2:1-18). From then until the end of 2 Kings 7, every episode centers on Elisha whose wonders often duplicate or echo those of Elijah. The recollection of his deeds by his sidekick, Gehazi (8:1-6), ends the first part. Elisha appears at both the beginning and the end of Part Two (8:7-13:25), but is absent from the narrative between. The second part focuses, rather, on the coups in Aram and Israel that were announced much earlier to Elijah (1 Kgs 19:15-17) and on the one in Judah that restores the legitimate Davidide to the throne. Part Three (2 Kings 14–17), though continuing the dual histories of Israel and Judah, manages to keep the spotlight on the North, on the expansion, instability, and, finally, destruction of Israel in contrast to the relative stability in Judah. Repeatedly the wickedness of the kings of Israel, compared to that of Jeroboam, the first defector from Davidic rule, is blamed for the divine wrath against the kingdom. In Part Four, (2 Kings 18-25), with Israel defeated, the narrative chronicles the story of Judah alone, explaining how despite the reigns of the two best kings ever, Hezekiah and Josiah, Judah too goes down to defeat. Here the tradition of divine promises to the house of David struggles against the historical reality of demise and exile at the hand of Babylon to forge an explanation for catastrophe grounded in covenant ideas.

Finally, a few words about translation. While I have consulted a number of translations, especially the New Jewish Publication Society translation and the RSV, my reading of the text derives principally from the Hebrew. As a result, all translations included in the text are my own. I have tried to avoid transliterated Hebrew, but have included it when an argument depends upon the sound of the Hebrew, the repetition of certain words, or the syntax of the language. For rendering of the divine name, I reproduce in English the unvocalized tetragrammaton: YHWH.

* * *

To write any biblical commentary is to stand upon the shoulders of giants. Still, it is a great privilege to add one's voice, however small, to the resounding chorus of reflection over the ages on a book that has meant so much to so many. Though I acknowledge in "Suggestions for Further Reading" the studies that I found most useful in my own work, let me single out for special mention the recent commentary of Burke Long and the literary insights of Meir Sternberg. Jerry Walsh, as well, generously shared his work with me. Closer to home my colleague and friend, Howard Marblestone, has been an unfailing source of wisdom and support. Last, and most appreciatively, I register my gratitude to the editor of the Berit Olam series, David W. Cotter, O.S.B. His patience and encouragement enabled me to persevere through unanticipated delays in the work, and his suggestions by phone, by e-mail, and over coffee in ʿEin Kerem proved practical and helpful.

At the end of the summary of the reign of nearly every monarch of Judah, the text of 2 Kings names the son who will succeed him. Yet before we learn anything about the son, the text generally shifts to the account of the contemporaneous king in the northern kingdom of Israel. In the gap thus created between the naming of the son and the delayed beginning of the story of his reign, there is space to hope that the son will do better than the father. So it is with us. In that hope I dedicate this book to my three sons.

Part One

THE STORY OF ELISHA
2 Kings 1:1–8:6

Chapter 1

ELIJAH AND THE DYING MONARCH

2 Kings 1:2-18

The book of 2 Kings opens with the penultimate episode featuring the prophet Elijah, whose tales occupy the last part of 1 Kings. In this final story of confrontation with a monarch, Elijah takes on King Ahaziah of Israel whose reign was introduced in the ending verses of 1 Kings (1 Kgs 22:52-54). There the narrator presents Ahaziah as a classic apostate following in the footsteps of his Baal-worshiping parents, Ahab and Jezebel. Here that apostasy is illustrated in a tale about the mortally ill Ahaziah attempting to procure an oracle from a local Baal at Ekron.

The artificial separation of this episode from the introduction to Ahaziah's reign resulted from the Septuagint's division of the Hebrew book of Kings into two parts. (The Jewish Hebrew text tradition continued to consider Kings as one book until the Bamberg Rabbinic Bible of 1516.) This division had the additional consequence of cutting off the last episodes of the story of Elijah from the others. Indeed, it might have made more structural sense to begin 2 Kings with the tale of the succession of Elisha in chapter 2. Yet since that tale, as well as several others, seem designed to claim continuity between Elijah and Elisha, perhaps no place in the text would constitute an entirely appropriate division. Compounding the abruptness of the beginning of 2 Kings is its very first verse, which seems unrelated to the story of Ahaziah and Elijah that follows it: "After the death of Ahab, Moab rebelled against Israel." In fact, the account of Moab's rebellion is not presented until chapter 3. Although the verse seems misplaced here, it does provide an image of looming trouble on the periphery against which Ahaziah's apostasy at the center appears all the more ominous.[1]

As it stands, the opening episode of 2 Kings serves several important functions. It looks backwards by providing a kind of summary of the personality and behavioral traits of Elijah.[2] At the same time it anticipates the vehement anti-Baal crusade to be taken up later by the rebel Jehu who dethrones and destroys the Omride dynasty. Furthermore, this tale is one of four in 1–2 Kings in which a prophet delivers an oracle to a dying king. As such it depicts Elijah in a "type-scene" associated with each major prophet in the book (Ahijah, 1 Kgs 14:1-18; Elisha, 2 Kgs 8:7-15; Isaiah, 2 Kgs 20:1-11), linking him into a prophetic chain.[3] I shall examine these functions in the analysis that follows.

Underlying the type-scene is an even more basic pattern in prophetic narratives that has been termed "prophetic inquiry." A king or his messenger requests an oracle from a prophet who delivers it, and soon it is fulfilled. Against this common pattern, this episode is distinguished by the threefold repetition of the oracle (vv. 3b-4, 6, 16) and the confrontations between the king's three captains and Elijah. These features suggest the following structure[4]:

---

[1] This verse is repeated verbatim in 2 Kgs 3:5, where it introduces the story of Moab's rebellion. Textual historians call this phenomenon *Wiederaufnahme,* "repetitive resumption." According to their hypothesis, the repetition is a sign that the material between the two verses is an addition to an earlier text. See Curt Kühl, "Die 'Wiederaufnahme'—ein literarkritisches Prinzip?" *Zeitschrift für die alttestamentliche Wissenschaft* 64 (1952) 1–11.

[2] See Alexander Rofé, *The Prophetical Stories* (Jerusalem: The Magnes Press, 1988) 33–7.

[3] As applied to biblical literature, the term "type-scene" was first employed by Robert Alter to designate an episode whose basic structure and sequence of actions is repeated several times in different places in biblical narrative, suggesting that each was created as a literary variation of a conventional scene. *The Art of Biblical Narrative* (New York: Basic Books, 1981) 47–62. For a study of the dying king episodes, see Robert L. Cohn, "Convention and Creativity in the Book of Kings: The Case of the Dying Monarch," *Catholic Biblical Quarterly* 47 (1985) 603–16.

[4] Diagrams included in this commentary are meant to expose parallel elements within an episode or a larger narrative section that create structural symmetry. Parallel elements are indicated by the use of a common letter and the "prime" notation (e.g., A, A'). Structural symmetry conveys meaning in a number of ways. In 2 Kings 1 the parallel sending of Elijah and delivery of prophecy represented by elements B, B' and C, C' focus attention on X, the confrontation between Elijah and the captains of the apostate king. The "A" elements provide a frame narrating the king's illness and death between which the action takes place.

A Ahaziah's illness and inquiry (1:2)
  B Angel of YHWH sends Elijah to messengers with prophecy
    (1) (1:3-4)
    C Messengers deliver prophecy (2) to Ahaziah (1:5-8)
      X Three captains confront Elijah (1:9-14)
  B' Angel of YHWH sends Elijah to Ahaziah (1:15)
    C' Elijah delivers prophecy (3) to Ahaziah (1:16)
A' Ahaziah's death (1:17)

A Ahaziah's illness and inquiry (1:2)

The episode begins with a "bang": a brief introductory exposition relates the fall of King Ahaziah through what seems to be a window lattice in a second floor room. Though his injury is not described, it is severe enough to prompt the king to seek a divine oracle to determine whether or not he will live. But the object of that request is not YHWH but Baal-zebub, a name attested only here in the Hebrew Bible, though referred to in the New Testament (e.g., Matt 10:25; 12:24). This name, which means "lord of the flies," may be a pejorative rendering of *baʿal zĕbûl*, (perhaps "Baal the Prince"), a common epithet for Baal in Ugaritic literature. If so, the writer not only signals Ahaziah's apostasy in seeking information from a foreign god, but ridicules the god as well by mocking his name. Indeed the use of the technical language of oracular request (*d-r-š be*, "inquire of"), in reference not to YHWH but Baal and the sending of messengers to his city, Ekron of the Philistines, underscores Ahaziah's apostasy.

B Angel of YHWH sends Elijah to messengers with prophecy (1) (1:3-4)

The narrator wastes no time in providing YHWH's response to the ill-directed journey of Ahaziah's messengers: a messenger of YHWH commands Elijah to intercept the king's messengers with a prophecy. The Hebrew verb form ("perfect") in v. 3 conveys a sense of simultaneity between Ahaziah's order to his messengers (*mal'ākîm*) and the divine messenger's (*mal'ak*) instruction to Elijah.[5] The oracle that Elijah is ordered

---

[5] Switching between two different verb forms, both of which express completed action, is one way in which biblical writers express simultaneity.

to deliver to the messengers is preceded by a rhetorical question, rich in the sarcasm that Elijah exhibited in earlier episodes. Here the geographical contrast between Israel and Ekron anchors the religious distance between YHWH and Baal-zebub. Further, the question, "Is there no god in Israel?," subtly echoes syntactically Israel's sarcastic plaint in the wilderness: "Are there no graves in Egypt?" (Exod 14:11). While the latter expresses the frustration of the newly released slaves, Elijah's gives voice to YHWH's anger at the king's desertion to a foreign god.

The formulation of the oracle in v. 4 calls our attention to a motif that will become increasingly important in this episode. "The bed which you have mounted *(ʿālîtā)* you shall not descend *(tērēd)* from," YHWH's words literally read. Control over physical ascents and descents symbolizes power and authority here. The tale opens with the king's fall from his upper room *(ʿaliyātô);* a stupid accident brings him low. Now YHWH promises that though he has "gone up" again, this time to his sick bed, he will not come down alive.

C Messengers deliver prophecy (2) to Ahaziah (1:5-8)

The text skips over the actual delivery of the oracle to the king's messengers, moving directly to their announcement to the king. In fact, their meeting with Elijah is conveyed not as it happens but in retrospect as they explain to the surprised king why they have returned. They report only that "a man went up *(ʿālāh)*" to greet them and ordered them to return to their king. Elijah's "ascent" here follows Ahaziah's fall, and heralds the divine power that the prophet will wield over this king. Then they deliver to Ahaziah the divine word uttered by YHWH's messenger.

Although the king gets the oracle about his future that he had requested, its source is not Baal-zebub god of Ekron, but YHWH God of Israel. As a result, he responds not to the substance of the oracle, which readers now hear for the second time, but to its bearer, "the man" whom his messengers do not identify. His request for information about the man's *mišpaṭ*, his manner and appearance, suggests that he suspects who has turned back his royal mission to Ekron. And when the messengers describe a hairy man[6] with a leather belt around his

---

[6] The Hebrew formulation for "hairy man," *baʿal śēʿār*, is found only here. Both its sound and its literal translation, "lord of hair," suggest an ironic contrast with *baʿal zēbûb*, ("lord of the flies") in the previous verse: on the way to *baʿal zēbûb*, the god of Ekron, the messengers encounter *baʿal śēʿār*, hairy Elijah, instead.

waist, he has no trouble making a positive identification—in reverse word order for emphasis: "Elijah the Tishbite is he!" (v. 8). Although the messengers do not know the man, the king recognizes him immediately as if there were but one man meeting that description. If so, why are the messengers not able to identify him? Is this hirsute and leather-bound character whom we readers know for his sudden appearances unknown to the royal court of Israel? The point seems to be the king's dramatic discovery of the power over against him. Though the reader knows that Elijah has been sent to turn back the king's messengers, their actual encounter is unreported. Then when they relate that encounter to the king, they cannot identify the man, only his physical appearance. The messengers' innocence serves the rhetorical purpose of placing the name of the prophet climactically in the mouth of the king. His certainty measured against their ignorance sets up the contest for domination between prophet and king that will now develop.

X *Three captains confront Elijah (1:9-14)*

Having heard the oracle prophesying his death and identified its agent, Ahaziah does not lie down to die. Instead he proceeds to pursue Elijah as if capturing the messenger will nullify the message. We must note, however, that his actual motivation for this pursuit is not disclosed either by the king or the narrator. In fact, Ahaziah's voice is heard only indirectly, as reported speech, by the captains he has sent to take Elijah.

The king's failure to control Elijah is dramatized by a sequence of three consecutive and repetitive scenes in which Elijah's power over the king is demonstrated. This sequence follows a folktale pattern in which successive scenes repeat the action of their predecessors, often with some intensification of the action, until in the final scene there is a climax or reversal.[7] Here the writer stages three confrontations between Elijah and the military officers sent by the king to capture him. The first two missions end in failure when Elijah calls down divine fire to defeat them, while the third succeeds, but on Elijah's terms.

The first scene (vv. 9-10) opens abruptly with the king's dispatching of a captain and his fifty men through whose point of view we see Elijah sitting atop an unnamed mountain. Only when the captain speaks in the name of the king do we know their mission: "Man of God, the king has said 'Come down!'" This brief command juxtaposes the two powers

[7] Alter, *The Art of Biblical Narrative*, 96.

pitted against each other in the confrontation: man of God and king. In his response Elijah throws his title back at the captain in order to demonstrate that it is an instrument of power greater than the king's: "If a man of God am I, then may fire from the sky come down and consume you and your fifty men" (v. 10). Against the king's order to descend, Elijah orders fire to descend. The narrator immediately reports the fulfillment of this oath without further comment. Clearly the point is not to dramatize the deaths of the hapless contingent but only to indicate the supernatural power of Elijah besting the military power of the king.

The sending of the second delegation is narrated in language identical to the first (v. 11) without indicating how the king knew of the fate of the first or what his reaction was to the deaths of his men. Instead the exact verbal repetition of v. 9 underscores the king's determination to capture Elijah at all costs. The only variation comes in the second captain's more intense putting of the king's demand. Instead of "the king has said, 'Come down!'" (v. 9), the second captain uses more formal language: "Thus says the king: 'Quickly come down!'" (v. 11). The intensification of demand is matched by the intensification of response, because now not just fire but "fire of God" descends to consume the captain and his men (v. 12).

The sequence reaches its climax in the third scene signaled by the narrator's repetition of the word "third" and by the very different approach of this third captain to Elijah. In only half a verse the writer conveys the humility of this nameless man both in behavior and speech. Unlike his predecessors he does not stand at the foot of the mountain and demand that Elijah descend; instead he ascends the mountain, bows on his knees, and begs for mercy. The description of this captain's humble bearing counters that of the king's mechanical repetitive sending. Presumably sent with the same mission, he does not deliver the message. He makes no demands of Elijah, only the request that he and his men not meet the fate of his predecessors. Framing his speech with a twice-repeated plea, "hold dear my life" (vv. 13b, 14b), he aligns himself with Elijah and not with the king who has sent him. The king's soldiers he calls "your servants."

B' Angel of YHWH sends Elijah to Ahaziah (1:15)

In response to this captain's humility the divine messenger now commands a second journey for Elijah, this time directly to the king. Not fire but Elijah descends at the command of the angel to go with the captain to the king.

C' Elijah delivers prophecy (3) to Ahaziah (1:16)

The text proceeds to the third delivery of the oracle, this time directly from Elijah to the king. In a complex sentence beginning with a motive clause, Elijah's oracle reviews the king's original misdeed and the misdirected journey to Baal-zebub, then repeats verbatim the oracle promising death to the king. The king, we should note, is both silent and unpictured. Now Elijah is in charge and Ahaziah is powerless before him. Elijah has come to the king at YHWH's, not the king's, behest, and the text records no verbal or physical response from Ahaziah. Earlier, from his messengers' description, he was forced to acknowledge that it was Elijah who had interrupted his mission. Now he is forced to face Elijah directly and hear the oracle that he had already heard second-hand. Only in death does he witness to the prophet's authority.

A' Ahaziah's death (1:17-18)

After all of the delays between the time the oracle was first enunciated by the divine messenger and the moment it is delivered by Elijah to Ahaziah, the fulfillment of the oracle is denoted by only one word: *wayyāmŏt* ("and he died"). Barely balancing the opening description of Ahaziah's injury (v. 1), this brief notice brings the tale to a rapid conclusion. Most important is the narrator's affirmation that the death was the fulfillment of prophecy. In this first episode in 2 Kings the theme of the authority of prophets over kings is sounded in a variety of ways: in Elijah's turning back of the king's messengers, calling down fire to kill his soldiers, and delivering an oracle to Ahaziah. Now the royal death is affirmed to be the enactment of the divine word that Elijah spoke.

The rest of the chapter, outside of the episode proper, records the regnal information necessary to proceed. The information that Jehoram succeeded Ahaziah because he had no son is interrupted by a notation dating this succession to the second year of Joram of Judah. The interruption is marked in the Hebrew text by a long space in the middle of the verse, a peculiarity of the Masoretic Hebrew text the function of which is not entirely clear. Here it may acknowledge the absence of the clarifying phrase, present in other ancient versions, "his brother," explaining why Jehoram succeeded Ahaziah.

Chapter 2

FROM ELIJAH TO ELISHA

2 Kings 2:1-18

After the reign of Ahaziah is closed but before the reign of Jehoram opens comes the story of Elisha's inheritance of Elijah's prophetic power. Only one other time, at the death of Elisha (13:14-21), does a tale stand outside the narrated time marked by the regnal formulas. This placement underscores the importance of the episode. This is the only account of a prophetic succession recorded in the Tanakh and, as such, it carries great ideological weight. In the midst of, but separate from, the sequential and interlocking formulas of royal succession, this episode again sets prophetic over against royal power. Furthermore, whereas royal successions are viewed as natural, this tale stresses the direct divine intervention that ends the career of Elijah and empowers Elisha. If monarchy claimed to mediate a divinely-given order to human time, the order represented by prophetic authority is superimposed upon it and supersedes it.

The episode is structured chiastically, its scenes mapping a journey and a return.[8] Elijah and Elisha proceed from Gilgal to Bethel to Jericho and then to the other side of the Jordan where the climactic ascent of Elijah occurs. Elisha then returns alone via Jericho and Bethel, and from there to Mount Carmel and Samaria. The first part of the episode makes use of the repeated sequence of actions—the 1-2-3-switch tech-

---

[8] A chiastic structure arranges the elements concentrically around a center, reversing the order of the elements after the central element. Thus here we get ABCDXD'C'B'A'.

nique—we just saw in chapter 1. For purposes of analysis we may diagram the story as follows.

A Elijah and Elisha leave Gilgal (2:1-2)
  B Elijah and Elisha at Beth-el (2:3-4)
    C Elijah and Elisha at Jericho (2:5-6)
      D Elijah and Elisha leave the sons of the prophets and cross the Jordan river (2:7-8)
        X The ascent of Elijah (2:9-12a)
      D' Elisha crosses the Jordan River and confronts the sons of the prophets (2:12b-18)
    C' Elisha at Jericho (2:19-22)
  B' Elisha at Beth-el (2:23-24)
A' Elisha returns to Samaria (2:25)

A Elijah and Elisha leave Gilgal (2:1-2)

The tale begins with the omniscient narrator's revelation to the reader of its climax: the ascent of Elijah. From this reader-elevated position, we are free to focus on Elisha's gradual coming to terms with the departure of his master. Not suspense but curiosity drives this tale: how, we might wonder, will this miraculous event take place and how will Elisha react to it? From the outset YHWH is named as the subject of this marvelous occurrence and the *sĕʿārāh* ("storm, whirlwind," a term often associated with theophany [e.g. Job 38:1]) as the agent of Elijah's ascent to the sky. This opening verse lends a numinous cast to the events about to transpire.

Having been informed in the first clause of v. 1 of the story's supernatural conclusion, we are returned in the second clause to the everyday, the beginning of the events that lead up to it. We see Elisha for the first time since Elijah chose him (1 Kgs 19:19-21) accompanying the prophet on a journey from Gilgal (probably north of Beth-el). The pairing of the two sets up the conflict between them in the next three scenes as Elijah insists that he journey alone, while Elisha swears to follow.

Verse 2 depicts the first of these encounters. Elijah commands Elisha to stay while he goes to Beth-el at YHWH's behest. But Elisha shows that he can invoke YHWH as well, as he takes an oath to remain with Elijah. This foreshortened scene ends with the narrator's elliptical notice of their journey together to Beth-el, indicating implicitly that Elisha has won the first round. Elijah's attempt to leave Elisha behind and

Elisha's refusal to be left raises the question of whether each one already knows where the journey shall lead. Does Elijah intend to spare Elisha the pain of seeing him disappear? Does Elisha intend to cling to his master until the very end? From their words, we may infer that what the reader already knows, each of them at least anticipates.

B Elijah and Elisha at Beth-el (2:3-4)

The appearance of the "sons of the prophets" *(bĕnê hannĕbîʾîm)* at Beth-el provides at least a partial answer to these questions. The "sons of the prophets" appear in the Elisha stories mainly as loosely organized groups of disciples bound to Elisha as their prophetic master. Here they greet Elisha on his arrival in Beth-el with the news, stated in the form of a question ("do you know . . ."), that YHWH will "take your lord from off your head." While the narrator "objectively" previews Elijah's ascent, the sons of the prophets describe the impending event in terms of its impact on their master Elisha. Elisha's reply closes the gap opened by his determination not to forsake Elijah by confirming our suspicion that he already knows what will happen. Elisha's admonition of silence to the sons, however, opens another gap: why the secret? Does Elisha not want Elijah to know that he knows? Is he concerned that if other people discover what is about to occur that they will attempt to prevent it? Is Elisha secretly anxious for Elijah to disappear so that he may take over the prophetic leadership? Verse 4 repeats v. 2, but this time we know that Elisha knows the score. This second command and refusal builds tension on the road to Jericho.

C Elijah and Elisha at Jericho (2:5-6)

The scene at Jericho repeats exactly the scene at Beth-el: the local sons of the prophets again inform Elisha and he again tells them to hush up. Again Elijah bids Elisha to stay put and again Elisha takes an oath of refusal. Only the last two words, "and the two of them went," hint that the repeated sequence of actions is about to be broken. After Elijah unsuccessfully tries three times to separate himself from Elisha, the narrator confirms his failure by referring to them as two together (cf. Gen 22:8). Whereas in the first leg of the trip the verb "to go" was used in the singular ("Elijah went," v. 1), here at the end it is used in the plural to signify the two prophets' common journey.

D *Elijah and Elisha leave the sons of the prophets and cross the Jordan River (2:7-8)*

At the end of their travel itinerary in the scene at the Jordan River the isolation of Elijah and Elisha is underscored. Verse 7 first sets fifty sons of the prophets (the number fifty echoing the number of troops in chapter 1) at an observation point "afar off." Then from their distant point of view the narrator depicts Elijah and Elisha paired again as "the two of them" (v. 7) standing at the Jordan. Silently we watch with the fifty as Elijah takes the mantle, which he once threw over Elisha, rolls it up, and casts it on the water. Clearly the narrator's description of the water dividing and "the two of them" (repeated for the third time!) crossing over on dry land is meant to evoke both Moses's parting of the Reed Sea and Joshua's crossing of the Jordan River itself. Only now Elijah and Elisha leave the land of Israel proper, and cross the border of normal human experience in anticipation of Elijah's remarkable departure.

X *The ascent of Elijah (2:9-12a)*

Verse 9 zooms in on the final conversation between Elijah and Elisha, out of earshot of the sons of the prophets. The Hebrew conveys the simultaneity of their crossing the Jordan with Elijah's request of Elisha. Although Elisha has never told Elijah that he knows what is in store for the old prophet, Elijah addresses Elisha as if he does: "Ask what I should do for you before I am taken from being with you." The event anticipated by the narrator, about which the sons of the prophets had warned and which was acknowledged to them by Elisha, is now confirmed by Elijah himself, though Elijah, unlike the others, does not cite YHWH's intervention. Moreover, Elisha, though never having discussed this eventuality with Elijah, does not feign shock or denial as he did in his three identical oaths. Instead, he has an answer ready, a request for two times the spirit *(rûaḥ)* of Elijah.[9] Did he demand the sons' silence because he wanted to be alone with Elijah in order to

[9] One midrashic tradition interprets this double portion of spirit as expressing itself in Elisha's performance of sixteen miracles, twice the number of miracles, by its reckoning, that Elijah performs. See Louis Ginzberg, *The Legends of the Jews,* vol. IV. (Philadelphia: The Jewish Publication Society, 1913, 1941) 239, and the discussion in Wolfgang Roth, *Hebrew Gospel: Cracking the Code of Mark* (Oak Park, IL: Meyer-Stone Books, 1988) 15–7.

make this very request? Elijah's response is even stranger, making the granting of the spirit dependent upon vision, upon Elisha's seeing Elijah depart.

After all of the build-up, the steadily rising action created by the journey to the Jordan, the repeated sequences of action, and the final conversation, the climactic scene is short and sudden. "Look (*wĕhinnēh)!* A chariot of fire and horses of fire!" Interrupting the conversation of the pair, the Hebrew *wĕhinnēh* indicates a sudden change in point of view, and the picturing of the surreal vehicle in advance of the verb "and they divided" creates an immediacy of vision. But whose vision? Is this a privileged view for the reader alone? Or is this what Elisha sees? Is it his point of view through which we see Elijah taken up in the chariot in the whirlwind to heaven? Only after he narrates the ascent does the narrator turn to Elisha's vision of the event. For now, we stand with the narrator watching the chariot and horses "divide the two of them" and lift Elijah to heaven in the tornadic updraft. Repeating in v. 11b the exact language of v. 1a, the narrator forms an inclusio, a sort of envelope, around the prospect and enactment of Elijah's ascent.

Now (in v. 12), reversing the normal verb-subject order by making Elisha the first word in the verse, the narrator shifts us to Elisha's point of view. With participial verb forms we are taken back to Elisha's reaction to the event just narrated. Telling us that "Elisha sees," the narrator confirms that Elisha has passed the test set by Elijah for inheritance of his spirit, though just what he sees is not altogether clear. And Elisha's exclamation—"My father, my father, the chariot of Israel and its horsemen!"—is ambiguous at best. What the narrator has shown us is not the "chariot of Israel and its horsemen" but a fiery chariot and horses. Does Elisha see the event in less supernatural terms as a kidnapping?[10] After his exclamation the text continues matter-of-factly from Elisha's point of view: "he did not see him any more." Or does Elisha see what we have been shown but simply express it differently? Does the vision awaken in him the realization that it is Elijah himself who is Israel's chariot, Israel's salvation? Later in the book fiery chariots surrounding Elisha will indeed save Israel, and the words of Elisha will be repeated by King Joash about Elisha himself. Without the context of later narratives, however, Elisha's words only deepen the mysterious atmosphere surrounding Elijah's translation.

---

[10] See Jack Lundbom, "Elijah's Chariot Ride," *Journal of Jewish Studies* 24 (1973) 39–50.

D' Elisha crosses the Jordan River and confronts
the sons of the prophets (2:12b-18)

In the next two scenes Elisha begins his solo reentry into the world which he and Elijah together had left. First we see his symbolic assumption of the role of Elijah in two ritual acts involving garments. His own cloak he takes off and rips, typically an act of mourning. But here the text specifies that he tears the cloak "in two," recalling the pairing of Elijah and Elisha, now ended. Next Elisha picks up the mantle (*ʾadderet*) of Elijah, which, we now hear, had fallen off of him. This small piece of delayed exposition nicely enables the writer to portray Elisha divesting himself of one identity and assuming another. Indeed the mantle symbolizes that *rûaḥ* (spirit) of Elijah that Elisha had coveted. With this mantle Elijah covered his face before God at Horeb (1 Kgs 19:13), enlisted Elisha in his service (v. 19), and divided the Jordan River. Like a relic, it transmits the power of the great prophet, so Elisha wastes no time in donning it and relying on it.

The trek back across the Jordan balances the scenes in the first half of the story. As Elijah struck the water of the Jordan with his mantle, so too now does Elisha. Yet here the narrator records a three-step process. First he strikes, then he calls upon "YHWH, God of Elijah," then he strikes again. Though the text does not say it, we are permitted to infer that the act of striking alone does not produce the intended result. Only after Elisha calls upon YHWH and strikes again, do the waters divide. Elisha's invoking of Elijah's name confirms to the reader that he has inherited Elijah's power. Note that the narrator never states this explicitly. He lets Elisha's actions demonstrate to the readers and to those in the story world that he is Elijah's successor.

Verse 15 shifts us from the point of view of Elisha ("and Elisha sees" [v. 12]) back to the perspective of the prophetic disciples with the opening word *wayyirʾuhû* ("and they saw him"). Initially it is not clear just how much they have seen: did they see Elijah's ascent or only Elisha's crossing? Their first words indicate that they have seen Elisha's dividing of the Jordan, for they recognize that he now bears Elijah's spirit. But their offer to search for Elijah suggests that the ascent of the chariot and horses of fire was beyond their physical or spiritual ken. From our reader-elevated position, their lengthy appeal to Elisha, suggesting what might have happened to Elijah, makes them look naive, childish. And just as earlier Elisha admonished them to be silent, now he asks them not to search. When Elisha finally breaks down under their continuing pressure and permits a search, it is only to humor them and to be able to say the equivalent of "I told you so" at the end of this contest of wills. Yet this exercise in futility does serve to cement his prophetic

authority and to end speculation about the whereabouts of Elijah whose
fate is never again mentioned.

In the transfer of power from Elijah to Elisha it is interesting that
YHWH does not take the stage directly, as he did for instance with Elijah
at Horeb. Instead we see the succession through the successively more
limited perspectives of the narrator, Elisha, and the prophetic disciples.
Elisha never tells the disciples what exactly he saw happen beyond the
Jordan; they must convince themselves that Elijah is gone for good.
Just as Moses' tomb was unknown, so too Elijah's final location was to
remain a mystery.

C' Elisha at Jericho (2:19-22)

The last two episodes that complete the chiastic pattern sketched
above are not, strictly speaking, connected to the tale of the succession
of Elisha. They are short miracle stories of the kind that we find elsewhere in the Elisha cycle. But in their present narrative location they
serve to confirm Elisha's power. In addition, their geographical set-
tings reverse the stages of the Elijah-Elisha trek to the Jordan.

In the first tale "the people of the city," in context Jericho, present
Elisha with an environmental dilemma that they expect him to resolve. They contrast the "good" living conditions with the "bad"
water that causes barrenness and miscarriage. Characteristically in
this type of tale the complainants do not tell Elisha what he needs to
do; they simply state the problem, and he enacts a solution. But he
does not act alone. He involves the people in the resolution by asking them to provide the raw materials that he needs. Here he requests
and they give to him a plate with salt on it, which he then throws
into the water source. He accompanies the act with a first-person
declaration by YHWH: "I have healed these waters; neither death nor
miscarriage will come from there again" (v. 21). In the last verse of
the episode the narrator builds a temporal bridge to his own day, explaining that the waters remain healthful because of the word that
Elisha spoke.

Although this is the first of the miracles that Elisha performs after
crossing from the numinous realm beyond the Jordan into the land of
Israel, there is no acclamation of his deed by the townspeople. The
prophetic disciples had already proclaimed that he bore Elijah's spirit
when they saw him from a distance (v. 15). Instead, this miracle effects
a transaction between writer and reader, a demonstration that Elisha
now bears YHWH's word and with it can do wonders.

While as Elijah's successor, Elisha is clearly paralleled to Joshua, who takes up Moses's role, this episode also establishes Elisha's link with Moses himself. For just as Elisha heals the water just after crossing the Jordan, Moses's first act after passing through the Reed Sea is to make sweet the bitter waters of Marah, also by throwing something (a stick) into the water (Exod 15:22-25). Both timing and technique work to make an ideological claim about Elisha's role in Israel.

B' Elisha at Beth-el (2:23-24)

The placement of the last episode, like its predecessor, seems governed more by its geographical setting than its subject. At Beth-el the first group of prophetic disciples came out to greet Elisha in section "B"; now at Beth-el in section "B'" Elisha is accosted not by "sons of the prophets" but by "little boys *(nĕʿārîm qĕtannîm)*" who similarly come out (the same Hebrew verb) to him from the city. Their repeated taunt, "Go up baldy, go up baldy!" hardly seems severe enough to warrant Elisha's curse. On the other hand, if their jeer is intended as an invidious contrast between the hairless Elisha and the hirsute Elijah, his anger is perhaps understandable. In any case, the episode provides an occasion for the writer to show the fledgling prophet calling down divine curse as well as blessing, hurt as well as healing. The power at Elisha's disposal is raw and amoral. Whether or not the bad boys of Beth-el got what was coming to them, the tale engenders in the reader a healthy respect for the authority of Elijah's successor.

A' Elisha returns to Samaria (2:25)

The verse with which the chiasm concludes charts the final leg of Elisha's itinerary from Beth-el to the capital, Samaria, via Mount Carmel, so closely associated with Elijah. It balances the initial journey to Beth-el (1:2) even if it does not end at Gilgal where the journey began. Nevertheless, Samaria is where Elijah had his last stand against Ahaziah and where the next episode begins.

Chapter 3

MIRACULOUS WATER IN
THE BATTLE WITH MOAB

2 Kings 3:1-27

In the two short episodes just concluded Elisha is shown offering aid and avenging insult, bringing life in one episode and death in the other. In the much longer and more complex tale to be considered here, he delivers both simultaneously as he is enlisted by two Israelite kings to save them and defeat the enemy Moab. Again water functions as an instrument of salvation for Israel, yet simultaneously the same water brings disaster for the Moabites.

This episode and 1 Kings 22 parallel each other closely in their initial sequence of actions. In both a king of Israel (unnamed in 1 Kings 22, though by context Ahab, and named only once, as Jehoram, here) seeks alliance with King Jehoshaphat of Judah to conduct warfare against a common enemy. Jehoshaphat responds favorably, and in the same words, but requests the intercession of a prophet of YHWH. The prophet (Micaiah in 1 Kings 22 and Elisha here), antagonistic toward the king of Israel, obliges after some argument and initially prophesies victory. From there the plots diverge, but the situations and structure are close enough to suggest that these are two versions of the same story, a "type-scene." Jehoshaphat's appearance in both is especially telling. In each case, his presence and alignment with a YHWHistic prophet sets a member of the house of Ahab in a negative light and thus voices a Judean perspective on northern Israelite history. A generally chiastic structure characterizes this episode:

Introduction to the reign of Jehoram son of Ahab (3:1-3)
  A First crisis and response: Moab's rebellion and Jehoram's
    alliance with Jehoshaphat (3:4-8)
    B Second crisis and response: thirst and the hope of a
      prophetic word (3:9-12)
      C Promise of resolution of both crises (3:13-19)
          Audience with Elisha (3:13-15)
          Elisha's prophecy (3:16-19)
    B' Resolution of second crisis: water comes (3:20)
  A' Resolution of first crisis: conquest of Moab (3:21-27)

Introduction to the reign of Jehoram son of Ahab (3:1-3)

Preceding the episode proper is the regnal resumé of Jehoram, delayed from 1:18 by the story of the ascent of Elijah and the succession
of Elisha. This placement not only loosens the numinous tale from normal regnal time calculation, setting it outside of standard chronology.
It also underscores the subordination of Jehoram and his successors to
Elisha, kings to prophet. Furthermore, Elisha's travels in the previous
chapter ended at Samaria, the city named once more in v. 1 as Jehoram's capital. Even though Samaria is typically so identified in regnal
summaries of the northern kingdom, here the name serves again to
subordinate Jehoram to Elisha: the text deals with Jehoram only after
Elisha's itinerary leads him to his city.

The information about Jehoram sets him apart to some extent from
his predecessors. Though an evildoer, he is contrasted with his parents. With this contrast the author alludes to the wickedness of Jezebel
who continues, we are subtly reminded, as queen mother as another of
her sons takes the throne. In particular, Jehoram is cited positively for
his removal of the Baal pillar, likely a votive stela, erected by his father,
Ahab. But this faint praise is immediately diluted by the formulaic reminder of his persistence in the sins of Jeroboam. As the founder of the
breakaway Israelite state that repudiated the house of David and the
house of YHWH in Jerusalem, Jeroboam is treated in these regnal summaries as the archetypal sinner. Though prophets like Elijah and Elisha
never question the legitimacy of the northern kingdom despite their
attacks on specific kings, the Deuteronomistic summaries routinely
view all of the northern kings as sinners like Jeroboam, simply by virtue of being his successors.

A First crisis and response: Moab's rebellion and Jehoram's alliance with Jehoshaphat (3:4-8)

The episode begins with a retrospective exposition about the annual tribute that Mesha, king of Moab, paid to the king of Israel. The inverted subject-verb word order and shift in the Hebrew verb form to the perfect indicates a repetitive action in the past against which the present action will take place. The incredibly high numbers of animals suggest Moab's complete vassalage to Israel. They also justify the revolt of Moab upon the death of Ahab. The Hebrew *wayyipšaᶜ be-* ("and he revolted against," [v. 5]) is used only here and in the account of Israel's revolt against the house of David in the time of Jeroboam (1 Kgs 12:19) to denote rebellion of one nation against another (with a different preposition it is used twice more to denote the revolts of Edom and Libnah against Judah [2 Kgs 8:20, 22]). Since, normally the verb expresses rebellion against God, its use here suggests the rupture of a long-standing relationship of vassalage.

Verse 5 repeats and resumes 1:1, as noted earlier. If, as some textual critics suggest, this sort of repetition points to the addition of new explanatory or midrashic material to an existing text, here the narratives about Ahaziah and Elijah's ascent would constitute such secondary material. On this assumption these tales mark time between the death of Ahab, after which the revolt breaks out, until Jehoram puts down the revolt. Since, according to the text, it was Jehoram and not Ahaziah who put down the revolt, it is only now that the story of the revolt and its consequences are narrated.

Nonetheless, by indicating in v. 6 that Jehoram went out and mustered all Israel "on that day," the narrator implies that the rebellion did not actually take place until Jehoram was king—two years after the death of Ahab and the intervening reign of Ahaziah—and that it met with an immediate response. That immediacy is also conveyed in the conversation between Jehoram and Jehoshaphat. Although the text uses a formula for commissioned communication ("he sent"), it has the kings address each other directly, eliding the role of messengers. Jehoshaphat responds to Jehoram's request for help with a formulaic and proverbial pledge of total support. Deriving perhaps from a formal oath of alliance, his pledge (v. 7), "What is mine is yours, my army is your army, my horses are your horses," (repeated from 1 Kgs 22:4) is delivered here without qualification or question. Nor does the route of attack that Jehoram chooses raise any objection from the loyal Jehoshaphat.

B Second crisis and response: thirst and the hope of a prophetic word (3:9-12)

The second crisis occurs at the end of a seven day march of the allied troops, now also including the king of Edom, enlisted, it would seem, because the battle route transverses his territory. After seven days the political crisis gives way to one of starvation: no water for the troops or the animals. A similar sort of enveloping of one crisis inside another occurs in the narrative of Elijah on Mount Carmel (1 Kings 18). There a calamity of severe thirst leads to the contest to determine the true god. Once YHWH is proven to be God alone, the rains come. Here the order of crises is reversed, and the supply of water precedes the joining of the battle with the Moabites.

In their reactions to this crisis, a contrast between the kings of Israel and Judah begins to emerge. The king of Israel (henceforth in the tale never referred to by name) immediately loses faith, blaming YHWH for the predicament and linking the lack of water to the impending defeat at the hand of Moab. Jehoshaphat, in contrast, seeks to turn to God, not away from him. His request for a prophetic inquiry elicits the news, not from the king of Israel but his servant, that Elisha is in the vicinity. By putting this information in the mouth of a servant rather than in that of the king of Israel himself, the writer subtly denigrates the king whose first reaction is despair. Elisha is here (v. 11) identified in two ways, by both his natural (son of Shaphat) and prophetic ("who poured water on the hands of Elijah") genealogies. But it is his link with Elijah that establishes his fitness for the task at hand.

C Promise of resolution of both crises (3:13-19)

AUDIENCE WITH ELISHA (3:13-15)

The text elides the kings' inquiry of the prophet and turns instead to Elisha's reaction to them. The contrast between the attitudes of the two kings revealed in their own words is now further developed in Elisha's response. First, Elisha delivers a sarcastic rebuff to the king of Israel directing him to "your father's prophets or to your mother's prophets" (v. 13). These words allude to the narrator's reference to Jehoram's father (Ahab) and mother (Jezebel) in v. 2. But whereas the narrator contrasted Jehoram and his parents, crediting Jehoram with removing the pillars of Baal, Elisha classes them together. Clearly the narrator's retrospective judgment is not shared by Elisha in the heat of the moment. Against the "factual" contrast between son and parents made by the narrator, the anger and the zealousness of Elisha stand forth.

In response to the king of Israel's pained reply, in fact a repetition of his frightened and faithless plaint of v. 10, Elisha further denigrates him by contrasting him with King Jehoshaphat whom Elisha respects. Although we and not Elisha heard Jehoshaphat's request for a prophet of YHWH in response to the crisis of no water, Elisha responds as if he knew that it was Jehoshaphat, and not Jehoram, who had made the suggestion.

ELISHA'S PROPHECY (3:16-19)

Elisha's oracle addresses both crises at the same time. Responding to the musician whom he summons, Elisha feels what the narrator identifies as "the hand of the LORD" and begins to prophesy. First he promises water to slake the thirst of man and beast. In a divine speech within a speech, Elisha first announces the result—a flowing wadi— and then the cause, the miraculous filling of the wadi with water in the absence of rain and wind. No natural happening this. The twice repeated verb in v. 17, "you will not see *(lō' tir'û)*," emphasizes the supernatural source of the water and contrasts with the earthly result: "you will drink, you and your cattle and your pack animals." From the prediction of what will be done for them, the oracle turns to what they will do, with YHWH's help, for themselves: battle and subdue the Moabites. Again the prophecy begins (v. 18) with the outcome, YHWH's giving of Moab to the allied forces, and proceeds with the means by which this is to be accomplished: the human conquest of Moabite cities and destruction of the trees, wells, and fields that support them. In but one poetic verse (v. 19) the text evokes a picture of total destruction:

> You shall smite every fortified city and every choice city,
> and every good tree you shall fell
> and every well of water you shall seal
> and every good plot you shall ruin with stones.

B' Resolution of second crisis: water comes (3:20)

The second crisis, addressed first in Elisha's oracle, is also the first to be resolved. The narrator links the coming of the promised water to the morning meal offering, thus suggesting its divine source. He does not linger to relate the eager drinking by men and animals that one imagines would have resulted. Indeed, he gives no attention at all to the allied reaction to the miraculous water. Instead he shifts our attention to the Moabite camp and the surprise consequences of the water there.

A' Resolution of first crisis: conquest of Moab (3:21-27)

In one verse (v. 21) the text shuttles not only across the border in space but back in time to review the war from the Moabite point of view. From his omniscient position the narrator replays the Moabite muster that took place some time in the previous week (cf. v. 9). Switching first to subject-verb (in the perfect) word order to express a past perfect sense, the exposition reports that the Moabites heard about the advance of the kings long before they saw it. Appropriately they respond to this hearing with shouting *(wayiṣṣā'aqû)*. In indirect discourse we hear the call to arms and finally see the result: the troops on the border.

After this glance backward, v. 22 begins in time just where v. 20 began, on the morning after Elisha's prophecy. But now we see the water from the point of view of the Moabite troops. Having already told us the real cause of the water, the writer creates dramatic irony by depicting it through Moabite eyes. "They got up early in the morning and, as the sun shone on the water, Moab saw from the distance the water, red like blood" (v. 22). Note that the sunshine intervenes syntactically between the two verbs predicated of the Moabites: "they got up" and "they saw." Though the source of the water is supernatural, purely natural circumstances confuse the Moabites and cause them to jump to a disastrous conclusion. The Moabites are shown as victims not of direct divine punishment but rather of their own impulsive reasoning. In the only direct speech in the scene the Moabites analyze the cause of the red water, jumping to the conclusion that the red is blood and that the blood has come from the internal fighting of the allied troops. Their final words, "And now to the spoil, Moab!" lead them to battle and the narrator to describe the battle that results both in the rout of the Moabites and, ironically, the withdrawal of the Israelites.

To describe the battle, the narrator abandons the Moabite point of view for a more objective stance, yet one that still represents an Israelite perspective. Rather than relate the Moabites' verbal reaction to their mistake, he simply describes the results in military terms: they smote, they fled, they pursued. The description of the destruction of the cities, fields, springs, and trees matches, and thus is made implicitly to fulfill, Elisha's prediction. Yet the fulfillment is not automatic, for ad hoc methods need to be used against one city that does not fall, Kir Hareshet (v. 25). As with the Moabites' false interpretation of the color of the water, there human error, here persistence brings about the completion of the prophetic word.

In fact the final conquest of Moab was not to be, despite the prophetic word. In v. 26 we are shifted back to the Moabite camp and to two efforts of the king of Moab to break out of the Israelite stranglehold. Through his eyes (*wayyar*, "and he saw") we first see the war going badly and then watch him send seven hundred swordsmen in an unsuccessful effort to break free. With the failure of this purely military move, the king turns to religion. As he "took" swordsmen, now he "took" his first-born son, his heir, to offer as a burnt offering on the wall. To whom he offers the son is not said; what is said is that his effort was successful in turning Israel back because of "great wrath." Whose wrath? YHWH's? That of the Moabite deity Chemosh? Does this ending attempt to resolve the clash between the prophetic tradition that promised total victory over Moab and the historical tradition that the Israelites withdrew? Although elsewhere the Hebrew *qesep* ("wrath") is used to denote YHWH's vengeance upon sinners (e.g., Num 18:5; Josh 9:20), here not Israel but King Mesha has sinned by sacrificing his son, so it would make little sense to announce YHWH's wrath upon Israel. On the other hand, biblical writers would not ascribe wrath to a god (Chemosh) whose power they would not acknowledge. Perhaps the writer's animus against the house of Ahab prevented him from ascribing a total victory to the king of Israel despite Elisha's prophecy. Or perhaps v. 27 is offered from the Moabite point of view, offering a Moabite perspective on the reason for Israel's withdrawal.[11]

---

[11] See Mordechai Cogan and Hayim Tadmor, *II Kings*, Anchor Bible 11 (Garden City, NY: Doubleday, 1988) 47–8, 51–2.

Chapter 4

MULTIPLICATION OF OIL

2 Kings 4:1-7

Without any transition whatever, the narrative veers from a war story involving all Israel into a series of four small-scale episodes in which Elisha performs miracles for individuals or his disciples. The first two involve women, one poor and one rich. The poor woman, abruptly introduced as the first word in 4:1, appeals to Elisha for help claiming to be the widow of one of his disciples. In her complaint she makes no specific request. Rather, she sets out her situation, twice referring to her husband as "your servant," thereby stressing the link between him and the prophet. Her words, "and you know that your servant was a fearer of the LORD," also are designed to appeal to Elisha's sense of obligation to a loyalist. Only after she establishes this relationship does she state the specific cause of her distress: the tax-collector has come to take her two children as slaves. Having lost her husband, she is now afraid of losing her children as well.

As in the earlier episode of the purification of the water (2:19-22), here too Elisha enlists the help of the person for whom the wonder is to be performed. He has her work with what little she has—a jug of oil—to make more. In fact, his question to her, "Tell me, what do you have in the house?" (v. 2), shows a less than omniscient man of God dealing with the woman on her own terms. This is a different image than that of the prophet pronouncing YHWH's word against the Moabite forces.

Moreover, in contrast to that public prophecy, this miracle is to be shrouded in secrecy. Elisha emphasizes that the multiplication of the oil must occur behind closed doors where neighbors, who have lent the woman their vessels, cannot see. Only the woman and her children are to participate in the oil-pouring. The miracle itself is denoted by participles, indicating the repetitive presenting of vessels by the children and pouring of the oil into them by the woman. This occurs in silence until there are no more vessels. At that point the woman breaks into dialogue with one child, now identified as a son, to request another jug, only to be told that there are no more. With the end of the supply of jugs thus highlighted in dialogue, the narrator then notes that the oil stopped.

Symmetrically, the scene ends as it began with the woman presenting herself before Elisha, now called a "man of God." But this time her words to him are not indicated, only his instruction to her. The focus is not on the woman's reaction to the multiplication of her oil, but on Elisha's provision for a destitute woman.

Chapter 5

REVIVAL OF A DEAD BOY

2 Kings 4:8-37

Against the background of the short episode of the miraculous provision of oil, the particular emphases of this much more developed
story are highlighted. There was a poor widow with two children but
no food; here is a rich matron with no children but plenty to offer Elisha. The poor woman appealed to Elisha; the Shunammite woman asks
for nothing. The miracle of the oil saves the poor woman's children;
the miracle of the Shunammite's child leads to his death. Elisha instructs the poor woman; the Shunammite takes matters into her own
hands and forces Elisha to revive her dead son.

This is a tale of surprises that catch both readers and characters un-
aware. Elisha, in particular, is twice caught off guard and must quickly
find solutions to the situations that confront him. Structurally, the main
act, the Shunammite's appeal to Elisha and his response, is prefaced by
three background scenes. Each of them begins with the phrase "one
day" and takes place against the situation set up by its predecessor.
The episode may be outlined as follows:

    I. Background
      A The Shunammite woman prepares a place for Elisha—
        "one day" (vv. 8-10)
        B Elisha confronts the woman and promises a son who is
          born—"one day" (vv. 11-17)
          C The son dies—"one day" (vv. 18-20)

II. Foreground
    A' The Shunammite woman prepares for her journey to Elisha
       (vv. 21-25a)
       B' The woman confronts Elisha (vv. 25b-30)
          C' Gehazi fails and Elisha succeeds in reviving the son
             (vv. 31-37)

A The Shunammite woman prepares a place for Elisha (vv. 8-10)

The first section opens not with the passage of time but with a particular day, the day that Elisha passed through Shunem and first encountered the woman whose character and behavior are at the center of the story. Although she is unnamed, she is called a "great woman," and by the end of this section we know why. Not only does she urge Elisha to stay and eat on this first occasion but she provides for him each time he comes to Shunem. Moreover, she declares to her husband her intention to furnish a guest room for the "holy man of God" for his use whenever he is in town. The initiative is all hers; Elisha asks for nothing and her husband does not encourage her. In fact, her husband makes no response to her generous declaration. Indeed, everywhere in the story he is defined in relationship to her: "her husband." Her "greatness" is also reflected in her recognition of the holiness of this man of God *before* he offers any demonstration of it.[12]

B Elisha confronts the woman and promises a son
who is born—"one day" (vv. 11-17)

By omitting any summary of how and when the guest room was completed or how often Elisha slept there, the text keeps the focus on the woman's initiative. Against this background, the second "one day" zeroes in on one particular occasion when, after taking advantage of the woman's offer, Elisha responds to her generosity.

Now a third person, Elisha's servant Gehazi, enters the scene with no introduction and no clue to his whereabouts during the time that Elisha has been staying in the woman's house. Elisha summons him as

[12] Interestingly, in a parallel episode in the Elijah cycle, a confession in nearly the same words comes from the voice of the widow of Zarephath about Elijah only *after* he revived her dead son (1 Kgs 17:24).

an emissary and intermediary to the woman to convey his appreciation and discover her needs. Apparent here is the distance that the prophet tries to maintain between himself and the woman whom he calls somewhat dismissively "that Shunammite" (v. 12) even as he seeks to reward her. Although Gehazi has called the woman and she "stood before him" (v. 12), Elisha addresses Gehazi and tells him what to say to her. His first offer she declines. By suggesting that he could speak to the king or army commander on her behalf, he again stresses the difference in status between them. But when she responds, "In the midst of my people I dwell," she exposes his offer as unrelated to her happy circumstance which calls for no special privileges. Moreover, although he addresses her through Gehazi, she responds to him directly, implicitly resisting the distance Elisha has tried to establish between them.

Elisha's repetition to Gehazi of his question, "So what is there to do for her?" (v. 14), elicits the first of several surprises that drive the action forward. Unbeknownst to Elisha and to the reader as well is Gehazi's news that the woman has no son. Suddenly we realize that we ought to have wondered about children, especially considering their importance in the previous episode. Just as quickly, Gehazi's words ("she has no son and her husband is old") evoke the "type-scene" of the barren matriarch to whom God miraculously grants conception. Yet no sooner is the connection established than the singularity of this tale against the background of those emerges. First of all, the Shunammite woman is not called barren; only her husband's age is blamed for her condition. Second, unlike Sarah, Rebekah, and Rachel, she is not defined in terms of her husband, but the reverse. She is the independent member of the couple who decides to feed and furnish and who acts on her decision. Furthermore, this woman is not even described as wanting a child and expresses no joy at Elisha's announcement. Finally, and most obviously, not YHWH but Elisha promises conception here. Perhaps these variations are meant to alert us at the outset that this promised child will be different from his promised forebears, that unlike the other children born through miraculous conception, this one is not destined for greatness.

For the announcement itself, Elisha speaks directly to the woman whom Gehazi has called, though the text notes that she "stood in the doorway" still at a physical distance from Elisha within. Both the words "doorway" *(petaḥ)* and the unusual expression "around springtime" *(kāʿēt ḥayyāh)* echo the annunciation to Sarai (Gen. 18:10) and again invite comparison to that episode. Indeed, like Sarai, the Shunammite expresses doubt at the possibility of childbearing, though, unlike Sarai who denies to God that she laughed, the Shunammite protests openly to Elisha, accusing him of lying. But the rejoinder to the woman's protest comes not from Elisha but from the narrator who immediately informs us that "the woman conceived and gave birth to a son." What is more, the narrator repeats and confirms Elisha's prediction of the date of birth.

C The son dies—"one day" (vv. 18-20)

As Isaac is no sooner born than nearly offered as a sacrifice, this child is born only to die. In two Hebrew words "and he grew up" the narrator summarizes his life against which the third "one day," the day of his death, occurs. Yet the author has chosen not simply to announce but to dramatize, however briefly, the death. Interestingly it is not at home with his mother but in the field with his father that the boy takes ill. The nameless boy's only words in the tale are said to his father— "my head, my head!"—who responds not with solicitude but with an order to a hired hand to take him to his mother. The father whose voice has been silent in the story until now absents himself as well from his son's pain. Nor is the mother shown to be actively engaged in tending to her son. No verb is predicated of her. We hear only that "he sat in her lap until noon and he died." Missing is the warm motherly affection predicted by Elisha—"and you shall embrace a son" (v. 16). Instead the mother is depicted with a receiving lap, not embracing arms. Only after his death does she become active (v. 22). With the death of the boy the real issue of the tale is joined: can the man of God revive the dead?

A' The Shunammite woman prepares for her journey to Elisha (vv. 21-25a)

No sooner does the boy die than his mother, silent in the previous scene, launches into action and speech. As in scene A, here too she seizes the initiative in relationship to Elisha. But whereas in that scene her motivation is clarified in her initial speech (vv. 9-10), here there is as much concealed as revealed until she speaks to Elisha directly.

While we might have expected her to weep or to rend her garments, the text depicts her purposefully laying the boy on the bed of Elisha, closing the door, and exiting. No words or thoughts accompany these actions, so we are left guessing about her feelings. She has deposited the boy's corpse on the bed of the one who promised him to her, but why?

Next, as in scene A, she calls to her husband, speaking the truth but now not the whole truth. From a reader-elevated position we hear her request, his question in response, and her evasive answer. Despite her seemingly powerful position in relationship to her husband, she must ask him for the means to take a journey and submit to his interrogation about her purpose. In her request she first makes light of her trip as a short and unimportant one: "that I may run to the man of God and return" (v. 22). But at the same time that she subordinates herself to her husband who alone dispenses asses and drivers, she conceals from him the reason for her journey, thus elevating herself above him. Although he expresses curiosity about the purpose of her request, he is apparently satisfied with her assurance: *šālôm* ("it is okay"). He neither asks about the condition of the sick boy whom he had just sent to his wife, nor guesses that there is any connection between the boy's health and journey to the man of God. As in the previous scene he appears insensitive, obtuse, disconnected from his son. He can understand going to a holy man on a holy day–Sabbath or new moon—but why today? Once the woman obtains the ass and the driver, she resumes control, saddling the ass herself and ordering the boy to drive without stopping until she says so. The journey itself is summarized in half a verse (v. 25a). Not the journey but the woman's preparation for it is the focus here. Her dealings with the dead son, her husband, and the driver reveal her decisiveness and her determination, though her exact motivation remains, for the moment, hidden.

B' The woman confronts Elisha (vv. 25b-30)

Like its counterpart, scene B, this scene of confrontation between the Shunammite woman and Elisha is told from Elisha's point of view. In the center of v. 25, the narrator shifts from the woman's perspective to Elisha's, and we watch with him as he sees her arrive. As in v. 12, he refers to her as "that Shunammite woman" (*haššûnammît hallāz*) and bids Gehazi to run interference as she approaches. Again, as in v. 13, Elisha's communication to the woman is recorded not as direct speech to her but rather as an instruction to Gehazi. From Elisha's repetitive question, asking about the health of each member of the Shunammite family, it is clear that he has no prescient knowledge of the boy's death. Yet to Gehazi, the woman replies with the same one-word evasion that she uses on her husband: *šālôm*.

Verse 27 resumes the description of her approach to Elisha, delayed by Gehazi's unsuccessful intervention, in the same words as in v. 25a.

Now the woman, who has not revealed her inner feelings, does so in body language when she grasps Elisha's feet, apparently thereby throwing herself to the ground. Her pain is expressed not first in language but in action. As in B, only after communicating once through Gehazi, does Elisha confront the woman directly. Now he actively prevents Gehazi from pushing her away; from her outer behavior, he perceives her inner state: "her life is bitter." But he still does not know the cause. The text critiques the power of Elisha by articulating his admission of ignorance and of YHWH's silence. Even though he is the "man of God," YHWH has not told him of the boy's death or the woman's grief. Just as Elisha did not know that the woman was childless, now he does not know that the child is dead. For her part, the woman responds indirectly by recalling Elisha's promise to her of a son and her reaction, but not speaking of his death. Her recollection takes the form of two rhetorical questions (v. 28) further denigrating the man of God by accusing him of having made a promise that she implies is now bankrupt. Although she never says that the boy has died, Elisha's subsequent actions indicate that he understands the situation.

But his response further lowers him in the reader's eyes, for instead of intervening himself, he sends the hapless Gehazi as his intermediary to revive the boy. Interestingly he orders him to travel in silence neither greeting nor responding to those he meets on the way. The woman, however, is not satisfied. Identified pointedly in v. 30 as "the mother of the boy," she ignores Gehazi and turns instead to Elisha to whom she swears an oath: "By the life of the LORD and by your life, I will not leave you." This oath recalls the one that Elisha swore three times to Elijah when Elijah attempted to leave the younger prophet behind (2:2, 4, 6). This intertextual echo is all that is required to explain Elisha's immediate reaction: "he got up and he went after her." Does her oath recall to him his own? So even as "Plan A," the sending of Gehazi, is underway, Elisha, in response to the oath, launches "Plan B," his personal intervention on behalf of the "mother of the boy."

C' Gehazi fails and Elisha succeeds in reviving the son (vv. 31-37)

Balancing unit C, the account of the boy's illness and death, unit C' recounts the boy's revivification at the hand of Elisha. First, however, the narrator describes Gehazi's ineffectual effort to revive the boy, parallel to the ineffectual effort of the boy's father in C to deal with his illness. The Hebrew subject-verb word order with the verb in the perfect tense subordinates Gehazi's attempt to the main action of Elisha. It has the sense of "meanwhile, while Elisha and the Shunammite were on route, Gehazi went off ahead." The narrator describes the lack of reaction by the boy to Gehazi's placing of Elisha's staff on his face with the same words that he describes the silence of Baal to the efforts of his prophets to summon fire from heaven (1 Kgs 18:26). Clearly this intertextual echo aligns Gehazi with those ineffectual prophets of Baal over against the successful Elijah and, by implication, Elisha.

Verse 32 resumes the journey of Elisha toward the dead boy. The narrator places us with Elisha as he enters the house and encounters the dead boy, conveying Elisha's point of view through the interjection *hinnēh:* "and behold, the boy dead and lying on his bed." Invited into Elisha's room, the reader, but not the mother or Gehazi, witnesses the miraculous resuscitation. Whereas the mother in C closed the door to this room behind her, Elisha closes the door from within. Though first praying to YHWH (v. 33), Elisha puts his body on the line, as it were, by seemingly attempting to transfer his energy to the dead boy. And it almost does not work, necessitating a second attempt. The narrator relates the two-stage process in some detail, conveying enticingly its magical quality. The first stage is "mouth to mouth"—and eye to eye and hand to hand: Elisha hunches over the boy to recharge his vital organs—breath, vision, and touch. When the boy's body warms, Elisha begins the second stage: pacing back and forth in the room. In both stages the narrator describes Elisha's final action with the unusual verb *wayyighar,* predicated in the Tanakh only of Elisha and Elijah (1 Kgs 18:42). Its meaning is far from clear, but it may indicate a final prostration over the boy which collects the energy that Elisha has created and transfers it to the dead child. Although Elisha prays to YHWH at the outset, the text records no direct divine intervention. The miracle is Elisha's, but neither his staff nor his "mouth to mouth" resuscitation were sufficient to bring the boy back.

Yet, despite his personal intervention to revive the boy, Elisha again summons Gehazi to convey the good news to his mother, again referring to her as "this Shunammite" (v. 36). Now the woman again falls at Elisha's feet, speechless before the man of God's miracle. She once exited (*wattēṣē,* v. 21) the room with a dead son within; now she exits (*wattēṣē,* v. 37) the room with the same son alive. Silent then as now, she carries with her the secret emotional life of joy, anger, gratitude, and resentment that her experiences have created.

Chapter 6

FEEDING THE HUNGRY

2 Kings 4:38-44

The two short episodes that follow the story of the Shunammite lack its depth of plot and character. They celebrate rather than criticize the authority of the prophet. Both are stories of food scarcity and supply in which Elisha's wonders transform impure into pure and few into many. Both begin abruptly with inverted Hebrew subject-verb word order signaling their independence from the preceding narrative sequence.

In the first (vv. 38-41), Elisha's disciples go out in the midst of a famine to gather one type of flora and come home with another, neither of which is otherwise attested in the Bible. If we cannot identify the plant which they sliced into the pot, apparently they could not either, "for they didn't know" (v. 39). In the climactic verse (v. 40) a sound play reinforces the problem of the episode: *wayyiṣqû* ("they poured") and *ṣāʿāqû* ("they screamed"). What was poured made them scream because it was poison and they could not eat it. Just as Elisha once threw salt into a spring (2:21) to purify the water, now he throws flour into the pot to detoxify the soup. The story ends with Elisha's instruction, "Pour for the people that they may eat."

In the second episode (vv. 42-44), Elisha gives virtually the same instruction—"Give to the people that they may eat." But this order, repeated after a servant doubts that twenty loaves can feed one hundred people, is followed here by a word of YHWH that Elisha utters to support his instruction. And the final verse confirms that YHWH's word was fulfilled. This episode, then, "corrects" the impression left by the first by depicting an Elisha issuing a parallel instruction but subordinating it to YHWH's word. This episode makes it clear that Elisha's provision rests not on his personal power but on YHWH's.

34

Chapter 7

HEALING A FOREIGN LEPER

2 Kings 5:1-27

Although at first glance 2 Kings 5 appears to be a single, continuous story about the leper Naaman, it is comprised of three distinct units, each focusing on a different character:

A Elisha (vv. 1-14)
    1. Naaman journeys to Elisha (vv. 1-7)
    2. Elisha heals Naaman (vv. 8-14)
B Naaman (vv. 15-19)
C Gehazi (vv. 20-27)

Unit A recounts the power of Elisha to cure Naaman's leprosy; unit B records Naaman's confession of faith in YHWH and its consequences; unit C details the efforts of Elisha's servant, Gehazi, to enrich himself at Naaman's expense and his resulting punishment by Elisha. Though at the end of each unit the story pauses, each subsequent unit offers a wider horizon from which to view the earlier action. Thus even though A concludes with the curing of Naaman, B proceeds to explore the religious dimensions of that healing. And C follows the fate of the departing Naaman at the hands of the jealous Gehazi and returns to the subject of leprosy.[13]

---

[13] The analysis here follows my article, "Form and Perspective in 2 Kings v," *Vetus Testamentum* 33 (1983) 171-84.

Naaman journeys to Elisha (5:1-7)

The problem of the tale, Naaman's leprosy, is related in the first verse, but the solution does not occur until v. 14. Between these verses we are led step by step alongside Naaman as he journeys from sickness to health. Although Elisha is not named in the first half, he is clearly the goal toward which Naaman moves, the plot's center of gravity.

The initial verse contrasts the fame and valor of Naaman with his disease: "Now Naaman, field-marshal of the king of Aram, was a great man before his lord and of high renown, because through him the LORD gave victory to Aram, and the man, though a valorous hero, was leprous." In contrast to the usual pithiness of biblical character description, here the praiseworthiness of Naaman gets signal attention. But the single descriptor "leprous" following the long list of attributes shocks us with the irony of Naaman's predicament. Furthermore, the careful description plants a number of key words and ideas, seeds that will germinate later in the narrative. The first verse thus acts as a kind of code, not deciphered until the story is complete. For example, the term "valorous hero" (*gibbôr ḥayil*), literally "man of substance," directs our gaze ahead to find out just what sort of substance Naaman is made of.

With Naaman introduced and the problem stated, the effort to solve it can begin. The journey to health is an indirect one, with Naaman arriving at Elisha's door only as a result of the words of intervening intermediaries. The first is a captive Israelite maiden described with terms parallel to those with which Naaman himself is described, thus strengthening the link between them and, perhaps, suggesting an unspoken divine urging behind her advice. While Naaman is a "great man," she is a "little maiden;" he a captain, she a captive; he is "before (*lipnê*) his lord," she "before (*lipnê*) the wife of Naaman." Despite her lowly position, her advice to her mistress begins the series of communications that will lead Naaman to Elisha. Skipping over the transmission of the message from Naaman's wife to Naaman and not repeating it when Naaman reports it to the king, the narrator simulates the lightning fast receipt of the news by the king of Aram.

After the king of Aram announces his intention to send Naaman with a letter of introduction to the king of Israel (v. 5), the narrator details the gifts that Naaman takes along, a seemingly unimportant detail which functions, however, as anticipatory of later events (v. 22). The momentum of Naaman's journey is maintained by the delay of the text of the letter until its delivery to the king of Israel. This delay as well focuses attention on the king's dramatic reaction. Intimidated by what he understands to be a challenge to *him* to cure the leper, the king of Israel explodes in rage against "this guy (*zeh*)," the king of Aram, and he rips his clothes at the blasphemous suggestion that he has healing powers: "Am I God to kill and to make alive?" (v. 7). The assurances of the Israelite captive about "the prophet who is in Samaria" have been sidetracked by an official royal memorandum sent from king to king but lacking any mention of the prophet. With this rhetorical question by the king of Israel, the writer mocks the impotence of royal authority. The apparent dead end of Naaman's journey is marked in the Hebrew with a Masoretic *pisqāʾ*, a blank space indicating here a full stop in the narrative motion.

Elisha heals Naaman (5:8-14)

When the story resumes, it is Elisha, now named for the first time, who initiates the action. Without benefit of an official letter, the prophet somehow hears of Naaman. Cutting through the royal red tape, he lets the king know who is really in charge: "Let him come to *me* that he may know that there is a prophet in Israel" (v. 8)—not "in Samaria" under royal patronage, but "in Israel" at large Elisha's power reigns. As elsewhere in the Elijah and Elisha tales (e.g., 1 Kings 21; 22; 2 Kings 1), the king of Israel is shown to be ineffectual; now he fades from the scene entirely. Though Elisha had addressed the king, it is Naaman who responds: "And Naaman came . . ." (v. 9).

Having summoned Naaman, Elisha does not communicate with him directly, relying instead on a messenger who relays the prophet's message to the leper standing outside the door. Naaman may have come like a conquering hero, "with his horses and chariots" (v. 9), but Elisha asserts his own authority by dismissing him without an audience. Having come so far to be "before the prophet," he is left instead standing at the door with instructions to wash seven times in the Jordan River.

The writer focuses on the discomfiture of the haughty, but ailing, field marshal by offering a rare biblical look into the thoughts of this, until now, silent character. Attention begins to shift from the cure to the mentality of the patient. First, Naaman reveals what he had expected from the man of God: a magical cure effected by Elisha's invoking of the name of YHWH and waving his hand (v. 11). Second, he reflects upon Elisha's actual instructions, not fathoming how the puny Jordan waters can have curative powers superior to those of the mighty rivers of Damascus: as a "great man" (*ʾîš gādôl*, v. 1), he had imagined a "great thing" (*dābār gādôl*, v. 13). All at once the blank figure of Naaman is shaded in, and we suspect that Elisha's instruction, in its simplicity, is designed to cure this arrogant Aramean of more than his leprosy.

Convinced by his servants, who, like the Israelite maid-servant at home, speak with the voice of wisdom, to swallow his pride and do as Elisha says, he is cured. The narrator records Naaman's compliance by repeating nearly verbatim Elisha's instruction, but adding the descriptive phrase, "and his flesh became like the flesh of a young boy *(naʿar qāṭon)*" (v. 14), in so doing, rounding off unit A in two ways. For one thing, the expression "young boy" forms an inclusio with "young maiden" *(naʿarāh qĕtannā, v. 2)*, appropriately, since it was her initiative that has resulted in his transformation. For another, he who is now described as a "young boy" was first introduced as a "big man" *(ʾîš gādôl, v. 1)*. On his way to a cure from leprosy, the big man was forced into submission to the prophet and transformed symbolically into a young boy. As he heeded the suggestion of the Israelite servant, so too he listens to his own servants. But though Naaman's leprosy has been cured, his attitude remains a mystery.

Naaman's conversion (5:15-19)

If unit A focuses on the healing power of Elisha, unit B centers on the spiritual transformation of Naaman. As his flesh "turned around" *(wayyāšŏb, v. 14)* and became clean, now Naaman the man "turned around" *(wayyāšŏb, v. 15)* to face his healer. Now he "stood before him" *(wayyaʿamod lĕpānāw, v. 15)* as the Israelite maiden had hoped at the outset *(lipnê, v. 3)*. Dialogue replaces one-way messages through intermediaries, a formal signal of a new relationship between Naaman and Elisha. Naaman's confession of faith in YHWH reveals that the physical healing has engendered an attitudinal change. Bitter arrogance has become reverent humility before the prophet and his god. The "lord" of the Israelite maiden has become the "servant" of the Israelite prophet. Though Elisha refuses his offer of a gift (literally *bĕrākāh* ["blessing"], v. 15), the offer itself establishes his new status in relationship to the prophet. With his monotheistic confession, Naaman implicitly acknowledges what the narrator affirmed at the outset (v. 1), that his victories were YHWH's doing.

Naaman's subsequent requests of Elisha go beyond confession to worship. With the first, the request for Israelite soil (v. 17), the writer establishes the reversal of Naaman's earlier attitude toward the land of Israel. Whereas before his "conversion" he denigrates the "waters of Israel" (v. 12), now he wants Israelite soil, presumably to use for an altar at which to worship YHWH. Repetition cements the change: because he confesses that there is no God "except *(kî ʾim)* in Israel" (v. 15), Naaman will offer sacrifice to no god "except *(kî ʾim)* to the LORD" (v.

17). The request illustrates the sincerity of Naaman's "turning," the first word and key theme of unit B.

The second request is a corollary of the first: Naaman asks advance pardon for appearing to acknowledge the Aramean god, Rimmon, when, in service to the king, he accompanies him to the temple. Ever the loyal servant before his lord (v. 1), Naaman appears as a marrano of sorts, forced to feign reverence to Rimmon (literally "pomegranate," probably a parody on Ramman, a title of the god Baal-Haddad), while inwardly remaining faithful to YHWH. This seemingly wordy request betrays careful chiastic shaping:

A For this thing
   B may the LORD pardon your servant
      C when my lord comes to the house of Rimmon to
          worship there
         X and he leans on my hand,
      C' and I worship in the house of Rimmon (in my
          worshiping in the house of Rimmon)
   B' may the LORD pardon your servant
A' for this thing.

The chiasm centers on the phrase "and he leans on my hand," denoting, perhaps, less physical than emotional support, i.e., "right-hand man" (cf. 2 Kgs 7:2, 17). Why this phrase should be so highlighted is not clear here, but becomes clear later in the narrative.

In contrast to Naaman's effusive confession and requests, Elisha's responses are brief; this is Naaman's scene, and he controls the dialogue. Elisha's refusal of Naaman's offer of a gift, though not explained, appears to follow from the theological perspective Elisha articulates: because Elisha attributes the healing to YHWH (v. 16), he takes no credit and will accept no gift. This perspective is underscored by parallel phrases that establish the line of authority: Naaman "stood before" (*wayyaʿamod lĕpānāw*, v. 15) Elisha, but Elisha "stood before" (*ʿamadĕtî lĕpānāw*, v. 16) YHWH. Then, to Naaman's two requests, Elisha replies simply, "Go in peace," not indicating specifically whether or not he grants the requests. Instead the two conditions of YHWH worship outside the land of Israel are allowed to stand without comment.

The scene ends with Naaman's departure balancing his arrival, as his "conversion" balances his cleansing. Yet with the leading information, "and he went some distance from him" (v. 19), the writer hints that the tale is not yet over.

Gehazi (5:20-27)

The departure of Naaman from Elisha makes room for a new character, Gehazi the "young man *(naʿar)* of Elisha" (v. 20), whose deceit sets the transformation of Naaman and the power of Elisha into a broader perspective. His appeal to Naaman elicits the man's genuine charity, while his lie to Elisha provokes the prophet's naked retribution. His actions are thus used by the writer to expose the depth of Naaman's "turning" and the impartiality of prophetic justice. Furthermore, the ignoble Israelite Gehazi serves as a foil to the God-fearing foreigner Naaman.

Gehazi's opening soliloquy (v. 20) discloses his deceitful plot to claim the reward which Elisha refused, launching dramatic irony that sustains the episode till the very end. Word repetition sets this character against others in the story. Whereas the "young maiden" *(naʿarāh qětannā)* wanted to help Naaman, Gehazi, the "young man" *(naʿar)* aims to exploit him. And while Naaman was concerned to support his lord with his "hand" *(ʿal-yādî,* v. 18), it is from that very hand that Gehazi wants to steal: "Look now, my lord has spared Naaman, this Aramean, in not taking from his hand *(miyyādô)* what he brought. As the LORD lives, I will run after him and I will take something from him" (v. 20). The centering of the phrase, "and he leans on my hand," above (v. 18) focuses the contrast between Naaman, who asks advance pardon for showing loyalty to his lord, and Gehazi, who excuses himself in advance for his treachery and criticizes his lord. With the derogatory epithet, "this Aramean," Gehazi impugns the man who has declared his faith in YHWH and who is about to act on it.

The soliloquy, finally, serves to set Gehazi against Elisha. Whereas Gehazi swears an oath on YHWH's name to take *(wělāqaḥtî)* something from Naaman, Elisha had sworn by the same oath not to take *(ʾim-ʾeqqaḥ,* v. 16) anything from Naaman. And Gehazi, furthermore, does not, like Elisha, call YHWH the God "before whom I stand;" Gehazi does not stand before YHWH, he "runs after" Naaman (v. 21). The immoral and secret intentions of Gehazi thus stand in opposition to the righteous and open refusal of Elisha.

Gehazi's subsequent behavior develops the character of the wicked Israelite over against the humble proselyte. His hot pursuit of Naaman is juxtaposed to Naaman's gracious reception. Alighting from his chariot to meet him, Naaman shows with his greeting neither anger nor fear, but rather concern: "Is all well *(hašālôm)?*" Ironically, *šālôm,* in its literal sense of peace and wholeness, is precisely what Gehazi intends to violate even as he responds *šālôm* (v. 22). Not only does he lie about the sudden arrival of two prophets to whom Elisha wants to give gifts, but he attributes the message to Elisha himself. Set in the pattern of a commissioned communication, this message is in fact fabricated. The "talent of silver and two changes of clothing" that Gehazi requests recalls the list of tribute that Naaman prepared for his journey (v. 5). Whereas Elisha refused Naaman when "he pressed him" (v. 16) to receive a gift, Gehazi, when similarly pressed (v. 23), packs up both what he requested as well as the extra talent of silver that Naaman offers him. Gehazi neither expresses thanks nor sends Naaman off "in peace" (cf. v. 19). Instead Gehazi's two young men "carry before him *(wayyiśᵓû lĕpānāw)*" the goods. This expression subtly alludes to the opening description of Naaman as *nĕśuᵓ pānîm* ("renowned," literally "of lifted face," v. 1) because of his victories. Here, in contrast, the young men "lift before his [Gehazi's] face" his own treachery. While Naaman's good reputation preceded him, Gehazi's crime is carried ahead of him.

Having committed his crime, Gehazi is shown moving swiftly to hide the evidence. With five consecutive verbs the narrator describes the cover-up: he came, he took, he deposited, he dismissed, they went (v. 24). As if to emphasize the surreptitious nature of Gehazi's actions, the direct object of the verbs "took" and "deposited," namely the silver and the clothes, is elided: "he took from their hands and deposited in the house." Gehazi's "underhandedness" is further emphasized through the pictorial image of "took from their hands." In fact, the conjunction of the words "hands" and "house" recalls the earlier pairing, "when my lord comes to the house of Rimmon to worship there and he leans on my hand" (v. 18). The word choice points again to the contrast between Naaman, who supports his lord with his hand in the "house," and Gehazi, who takes from Naaman's hands and uses his house to betray his lord, Elisha.

In the final scene (vv. 25-27) the dramatic irony of unit C is resolved as Gehazi is undone. Indeed, the main issues of all three units of the narrative conjoin in this resolution. Elisha once again exercises his power, this time not to cure (A), but to curse and punish the deceitful Gehazi (C) for his crime against the righteous Naaman (B). Elisha's confrontation of Gehazi rings with irony. With Gehazi's "young men" gone, the now unnamed "he" comes and stands "opposite" his lord, not "before" him as had Naaman in relation to both the king of Aram (v. 1) and Elisha himself (v. 15). This confrontational posture anticipates Elisha's curt query: "Where from, Gehazi?" To Gehazi's evasive comment, Elisha replies bitterly (v. 26), juxtaposing Naaman's kindness ("the man descended from his chariot to greet you") with Gehazi's greed ("to take silver and to take garments"). In fact, Elisha exaggerates Gehazi's crime by listing far more than he took or was offered: "olive trees and vineyards, and flocks and herds, and menservants and maidservants." This laundry list of stolen possessions recalls Samuel's warning of what a despotic king will take from his people (1 Sam 8:14-17). Here they associate Gehazi's crime with the worst excesses of corruption. Elisha's curse is the fitting *quid pro quo,* for having stolen Naaman's possessions, Gehazi now inherits his disease as well. The concluding words, "leprous like snow," repeat and intensify the last word in the introductory verse ("leprous," v. 1) and thus serve as a final *inclusio.*

Though maligned by Gehazi, Naaman emerges as a servant of Elisha more loyal than Gehazi, whom Elisha condemns. Naaman becomes what Elisha calls simply "a man" (v. 26), any man who turns to YHWH. Not only does the prophet accept the loyalty of outsiders; he also punishes the disloyalty of insiders. Thus the Gehazi episode draws the story of Naaman into a larger arena by spotlighting the universal standard by which Elisha and, by implication, YHWH judge foreigners and Israelites.

Chapter 8

DIVINING A BORROWED TOOL

2 Kings 6:1-7

This episode continues the pattern of following a long and complex episode with one or two short and simple ones. This tale bears the same spirit as those preceding the Naaman story, in particular the account of the poisoned pot (4:38-41). Both begin with Elisha surrounded by his disciples, "the sons of the prophets," who face a problem—hunger or housing—that needs a solution. In the process of solving the problem, a new crisis arises which Elisha resolves by literally throwing something at it.

No introductory exposition sets the background for the episode; instead the disciples articulate their housing problem to Elisha, who accepts their suggestion to cut timber and build a new house near the Jordan River. That location constitutes the only link between this episode and the preceding story of Naaman. The key word here is *hammāqôm*, "the place." The disciples complain that their current *māqôm* (v. 1) is too small and receive Elisha's blessing to build a new *māqôm* (v. 2). Yet our attention is soon shifted to the *māqôm* in the water where the axe-head went under (v. 6). At the same time, one particular disciple ("the one") is differentiated from the group. He first pleads with Elisha to accompany them and then cries out to him when his borrowed axe-head sinks in the Jordan. Elisha's presence turns out to be providential, for he is able to recover the axe-head by throwing a stick in the water and making the axe-head float. As nearly always in these accounts, the tale ends when Elisha issues an order to the recipient of the miracle— to sell the oil and pay your debt, to pick up your son, to eat—here, to "lift it (the axe handle) up." The recipient does as Elisha says and goes off without a word. The focus is on the man of God and the miracle rather than on the gratitude of the recipient.

Chapter 9
DIVERTING THE ARAMEAN ARMY
2 Kings 6:8-23

In this longer episode, and the still longer one following it, Elisha is again a player, indeed the pivotal player, on the international military front. Verse 8 reintroduces the anonymous king of Aram, who had sent Naaman to Elisha, continuing to battle against Israel. So we discover belatedly that the raid in which the Israelite woman who became Naaman's wife's servant was captured was not an isolated incident, but part of Aram's ongoing aggression against Israel. The short incident in 6:1-6 functions, in retrospect, as a time-filler between two encounters of Aram and Israel. At the same time, 6:8-23 is verbally linked to 6:1-6 by its initial focus on the *māqôm* (repeated three times in 6:8-10) where the Arameans are encamped and which Elisha warns the king of Israel to avoid. Discoveries both visual and intellectual suggest the following chiastic structure for this episode.

A Expositional antecedent: Aramean raids on Israel thwarted
   by Elisha's insight (6:8-10)
   B The king of Aram is made aware of Elisha's insight
      (6:11-14)
      C YHWH opens the eyes of Elisha's servant (6:15-17)
         X YHWH blinds the Aramean army and takes it to
            Samaria (6:18-19)
      C' YHWH opens the eyes of the Aramean army (6:20)
   B' The king of Israel sees, feasts, and dispatches the Aramean
      army (6:21-23a)
A' Expositional consequence: Aramean raids cease (6:23b)

A Expositional antecedent: Aramean raids on Israel thwarted by Elisha's insight (6:8-10)

The episode begins with an exposition that explains how Elisha repeatedly prevented the Israelite army from being caught by Aramean raiders. Beginning with inverted word order to indicate a habitual situation, the narration opens into not actual but typical dialogues—first between the king of Aram and his officers and then between Elisha and the king of Israel. That these are habitual, not singular, occasions is made clear by the speakers' vague references to "such and such a place" (v. 8) and "this place" (v. 9). In each case only one party speaks (king of Aram and Elisha) and the effect is that they speak to each other, or rather, past each other as Elisha enables the Israelite troops to avoid encountering their enemy. The background exposition ends as the narrator stresses again Elisha's repeated intervention: "not once and not twice" (v. 10).

B The king of Aram is made aware of Elisha's intervention (6:11-14)

Against this backdrop, the action proper begins in v. 11 when the king explodes in rage and his servants reveal to him the cause of his military failures. First given a privileged view of the king's inner state ("and the king's heart stormed"), we then see his naiveté in assuming that a traitor in his ranks has revealed his whereabouts to the king of Israel. Not until he asks does an officer tell him about Elisha, as if it is common knowledge to everyone but the king. The king of Aram is represented to be "out of the loop," needing instruction from his servants as he did in the case of Naaman. With a ribald touch the servant emphasizes Elisha's uncanny knowledge by his hyperbolic claim that Elisha knows what goes on in the king's bedroom! In this short scene the author offers an inside view of the palace in Aram: the frustration of the king, and the servants having a laugh at his expense, finally revealing to him what they have known all along. And though he huffs and puffs, ordering a search party to find Elisha, no search is reported, only the information that Elisha is in Dothan. The king's overreaction is also manifested in the size and composition of the military expedition that he sends to capture the prophet: "horses and chariots and a strong force" (v. 14). Although in this scene the king comes to recognize that it is Elisha who has interfered with his battle plans, his reaction exposes his ignorance of the actual power of the prophet.

C *Y*HWH *opens the eyes of Elisha's servant (6:15-17)*

With v. 15 the scene changes to Dothan and the point of view to that of Elisha's servant. Through the servant's eyes we see the Aramean forces surrounding the city early the next morning. To his anguished question, "Woe, lord, how will we make it?" Elisha counsels, "Have no fear." Disconsolate, the servant points to the obvious reality: there are more of them than of us (v. 16). To answer this plaint Elisha appeals to a higher authority. His prayer to YHWH is answered when YHWH offers the servant second sight. Now, again through the servant's eyes, newly opened, we see "horses and chariots of fire surrounding Elisha" (v. 17). This vision echoes the supernatural image that accompanied Elijah in his departure from Elisha. The repetition of the motif here forges another link between Elijah and Elisha and further signifies the inheritance by Elisha of Elijah's mantle.

X *Y*HWH *blinds the Aramean army and takes it to Samaria (6:18-19)*

If Elisha, servant, and reader now see the counterforce, the Aramean army cannot, for they "came down against him" (v. 18). Now Elisha prays to YHWH a second time, not for sight but for sudden blindness (a condition reported only one other time in the Bible, striking the men of Sodom and Gomorrah [Gen 19:11]) to smite the Arameans. Here, at the literary center of the episode, Elisha strikes the blow that decisively stymies the Aramean intentions. Again the narrator takes pains to confirm that YHWH directly answers Elisha's prayer. The confusion of the Arameans at the hand of YHWH is shown in the ease with which Elisha leads them to Samaria, claiming "this is not the way and this is not the city" (v. 19). With dramatic irony he promises to lead them to the man they want.

C' *Y*HWH *opens the eyes of the Aramean army (6:20)*

As Elisha prayed that his servant see the reality of the supernatural troops surrounding him, now, in the parallel section, he prays again to YHWH that the Aramean army see where it really is. With the third use of *hinnēh*, we see them see themselves in Samaria before both Elisha, "the man [they] wanted," and the king of Israel. They are granted neither speech nor action, thus underscoring their powerless status in the hands of Elisha and YHWH.

B' The king of Israel sees, feeds, and dispatches the Aramean army (6:21-23a)

Balancing the scene between the king of Aram and his servants (B), this scene features the king of Israel and Elisha. In each case the king harbors an assumption that must be overturned. Earlier, the king of Aram needed to be disabused of his belief that there was a traitor in his midst. Here, having been handed his enemy on a platter, the king of Israel assumes that he should destroy them, and he minces no words in asking Elisha permission to do so. But just as the servants of the king of Aram reverse his expectations by fingering Elisha as the source of his problems, Elisha counsels not killing but feasting for the Aramean enemy. The logic of his argument has less to do with humanitarian considerations than it does with the logic of retribution. Because it was not the king who took the Arameans captive with his own sword and bow, risking his life and that of his troops, he has no claim on their lives. Rather, as visitors delivered by Elisha, they deserve to be fed and sent home. Again we see Elisha as provider, indirectly here, of food and drink for those in need, even enemies. For his part, the king of Israel follows Elisha's instructions without question, reflecting the subordination of king to prophet repeatedly illustrated in the Elisha cycle.

A' Expositional consequence: Aramean raids cease (6:23b)

The last half-verse returns to the expositional perspective of the introduction explaining the historical situation that existed as a result of the episode just narrated. It provides a short end-of-story frame.

Chapter 10

ENDING THE SIEGE OF SAMARIA

2 Kings 6:24-7:20

The next Elisha story begins with a reversal of the conditions just established. There Elisha's generosity to the Aramean troops is reported to have reaped peace in return (v. 23). Here the Arameans, under a now named King Ben-hadad, invade again, besieging Samaria and causing a severe famine. Although the episode centers on Elisha's prophecy of the end of the famine and its fulfillment, it arrives at its conclusion only by way of two short stories. The first exposes the impotence of the highest, Israel's king; the second the surprising discovery by four lepers, society's lowest. The confrontation between king and prophet is enveloped by the two stories, and they are framed in turn by narrations of background and consequence.

> A Background: Siege and famine (6:24-25)
> > B A story illustrating the horrors of famine (6:26-31)
> > > C Elisha prophesies to the king and his aide the end of famine and the death of the aide (6:32-7:2)
> > B' A story explaining how the siege and famine were ended (7:3-16)
> A' Conclusion: Confirmation of Elisha's prophecy of the death of the aide (7:17-20)

A Background: Siege and famine (6:24-25)

With only the loosest link to the previous episode, "And so it was, after this . . ." the narrator proceeds to set the stage for a new tale involving the Arameans, Israelites, and Elisha. Although the preceding tale ends with the comment that Aramean raids had ended, the narrator now reports that King Ben-hadad had besieged Samaria with all of his army. No explanation for the change in Aramean policy is given, though the oath that the king of Israel swears against Elisha below (v. 31), heard against the previous episode, suggests that he blames the prophet's leniency toward the Aramean troops for the current crisis.

Like v. 24, v. 25 begins with *wayĕhî*, "and so it was," continuing the description of the background situation. The depth of the famine caused by the siege is illustrated in economic terms. Utterly useless and revolting items, a donkey's head and "dove's dung" (perhaps the popular name of inedible husks of plants) are going for outrageously high prices.

B A story illustrating the horrors of famine (6:26-31)

From the general background we move to a particular tale, a parable of sorts, that shows the king powerless before the famine and before a woman who comes to him for judgment. Beginning like the two previous verses with *wayĕhî* and framed by the repeated participial clause, "the king [he] is walking on the city wall" (vv. 26, 30), this tale occupies a temporal niche somewhere between background and the narrative present of the story. Though it is a specific incident, the participial framing suggests a typical situation, a story illustrative of the depths to which the population is reduced and of the frustration of the king who can only pace the city walls.

The woman's appeal to the king may be read as a version of a type-scene reflected also in the appeal of the woman of Tekoa to David (2 Sam 14:4-5) and of the two prostitutes to Solomon (1 Kgs 3:16-28). Like the woman of Tekoa, she begins with the formal language of appeal: "Help, my lord the king!" But here the king is pacing atop the wall, not sitting in his palace receiving petitioners. He responds at first not with a proper invitation for her to state her case, but rather with frustration and sarcasm: "No! Let the LORD help you! Where can I get help for you? From the threshing floor or the winepress?" (v. 27). Only after he vents his anger at the poor woman does he regain his royal composure and properly ask what she wants ("What is it?" [v. 28]). Then he hears that the situation is far worse than he thinks.

Like the prostitute before Solomon, the woman seeks justice, but a terribly perverted justice. Having shared her own son for dinner with another mother, she now demands that the woman fulfill her promise

and cannibalize her son as well. The depths of the horror come through
in the woman's utter lack of self-consciousness about the crime she has
committed and by her expectation that the king would take her side.
Whereas one of the prostitutes before Solomon pleaded for the life of
her son, this woman asks for the death of the other woman's son. And
whereas the judicious Solomon exposed the true mother of the living
son, here Jehoram offers no solution. He responds not with words but
action, by tearing his coat in mourning. Unlike Solomon the wise, Jehoram is reduced to silence by the request and the situation. Nor does
the narrator comment on the calamity. Instead he reports from the perspective of the people their view of the king wearing sackcloth beneath
his torn garments (v. 30).

The king's oath (v. 31), in which he vows revenge against Elisha
brings the prophet's name into the story for the first time. Coming outside of the frame provided by the repeated clause, "the king was walking on the city wall," it nonetheless derives its meaning from the story
within the frame. The king blames Elisha for the siege and the famine
and so vows to have his head by day's end. This blame makes sense
only in light of the previous episode in which Elisha urged the king,
against his own inclination, to send the Aramean troops home well-
fed. Now those troops have returned to bring Israel the misery illustrated by the case of the cannibal mothers.

C Elisha prophesies to the king and his aide the end of the famine and the death of the aide (6:32-7:2)

With the king's naming of Elisha, the story shifts to the prophet's
house. The twice repeated participle "sitting" evokes the calm setting
into which the narrative present now moves. In a complicated temporal sequence the narrator first informs us somewhat ambiguously, "He
sent a man before him." But before the man arrives, Elisha clairvoy-
antly asks the elders rhetorically if they have not seen that the king has
sent a messenger to cut off his head. And no sooner does he tell them
to close and hold fast the door against him than the messenger (or the
king, depending on whether or not one amends the text) appears. The
effect is of a sudden rush into the prophetic calm, with action and prediction overtaking each other.

But though the king swore to have Elisha's head, upon seeing the
prophet, the king expresses his despair instead. In response, Elisha issues an oracle in YHWH's name that, like the narrator's initial description of the results of the famine (v. 25), is expressed in economic terms.

In contrast to the "today" of the story, when repulsive items fetch exorbitant prices, tomorrow flour and barley will be cheap, Elisha predicts. And to the sarcastic skepticism of the king's aide, Elisha offers a follow-up oracle promising, in effect, that though he will see the break in the famine, he will not live to share in it. So the king's original intention to have Elisha's head is unfulfilled; instead it is Elisha who apparently will have revenge on the doubting aide.

B' A story explaining how the siege and the famine were ended (7:3-16)

A comic tale backs into the fulfillment of Elisha's oracle. The scene shifts to a group of four lepers outside the city gate of Samaria pondering their fates. Initially there appears to be no connection between this scene and what has come before. But, as the tale progresses, the gap opened up by the sudden appearance of the lepers is closed, and their instrumentality in ending the famine is revealed.

Inverted subject-verb word order signals a new scene that starts narrated time afresh in a new location. Like the previous scene in Elisha's house, this one begins with the principals sitting *(yošbîm)* and talking. Though lepers and hence outcasts, they hatch a plan far more rational than that of the cannibal mothers. In contrast to the after-the-fact rationalization of the mother, this plan (vv. 3-4) makes sense: if death from starvation awaits in the city or outside of it, there is nothing to lose by deserting to the Arameans.

Action begins in v. 5 when the narrator tells of the lepers' twilight walk to the edge of the Aramean camp. There the interjection *hinnēh* ("behold") shifts us into their point of view: "no man is there." At this point, instead of recording their reaction to this surprise, the narrator explains what has become of the Arameans. He keeps us in suspense about the lepers at the same time that he closes the gap opened by their surprising discovery. Flashing back to the scene in the Aramean camp some time earlier, the narrator omnisciently portrays the divine intervention that caused the Arameans to flee. As in the earlier tale of the Arameans surrounding Elisha (6:15-17), the motif of the supernatural army represents YHWH's presence. There sight, here sound achieves the desired effect. Hearing the sounds of chariots, horses, and soldiers, the Arameans determine that Israel has hired a powerful alliance to come against them. That they should imagine not Judahites or Edomites but rather Hittites and Egyptians testifies to the power of YHWH to throw Israel's enemy into total disarray. Only in v. 7, after the report of their flight, do we hear exactly when it occurs: during the very same twilight hours—clearly, only minutes before the lepers' arrival. By reserving this information until now, the narrator augments the sense of divine control of the whole situation. Had the lepers left the city gate much earlier they would not have found an empty camp. Emphasized too is the haste of the Arameans' departure, measured by what they left behind (v. 7), and preparing us for what the lepers are to find.

Verse 8 resumes (in another example of *Wiederaufnahme*) the scene interrupted by the flashback by repeating nearly verbatim the last clause before it (v. 8; cf. v. 5): "And these lepers came to the edge of the camp." Thanks to the flashback, we know more than the lepers and so can read of their reaction with a mixture of curiosity and amusement. Whereas earlier the lepers reflected and then acted, here they act first and only afterwards talk about what they should do. In v. 8 a burst of verbs suggests the speed and purpose with which they set upon the spoils: they came, ate, drank, took, went, hid, went back, came, took, went, hid. After slaking their hunger and thirst, they proceed to the goods, interestingly the same items—silver, gold, and garments—that Naaman brought with him from Aram to Israel as tribute. Only after gathering two tents' worth of hidden treasures, do they stop for breath.

With the same reflective and rational frame of mind as at the outset (and made parallel by the narrator's identical stage direction, "and each one said to the other"), they analyze their new situation. Concerned first with the broad moral issue ("It's not right what we are doing") but finally with their own culpability as well ("we shall incur guilt"), they determine to apprise the palace of their discovery. So they return to the city gate whence they came, and we, along with the gatekeepers, hear from their point of view what they have found. They describe the tethered horses and asses and undisturbed tents, though they omit their own plundering and hiding of silver and gold. They describe only what they saw; they do not speculate about the fate of the Aramean army.

Their information launches the king into action still the very same night (v. 12). Now he offers an explanation for the deserted Aramean camp. Unlike the lepers who, in their explanation, stick to what they have seen, the king, who has seen nothing, presumes to analyze Aramean strategy just as his Aramean counterpart speculated about Israelite intelligence in the previous episode. He blusters, "Let me tell you (*ʾagîdāh-nā lākem*) what Aram has done to us" (v. 12) and describes their plans for an ambush, even imagining their conversation. His worries ring hollow against our privileged knowledge of the Arameans' actual conversation (v. 6).

As so often in the Elisha tales, a servant speaks up with the voice of reason (v. 13). Poking a pin into the king's bluster, he says with the same reasoning as the lepers that we lose nothing by investigating. Belatedly, the king agrees and sends out an intelligence team. Their discoveries of the roadside remains of the Arameans' hasty exodus fill the gap opened by the narrator's report of the Aramean flight (v. 7). From the scouts' point of view (*wěhinnēh*, v. 15), we see the discarded clothes and vessels of the Aramean army, certain evidence of their abandonment of the siege.

By now we have viewed the Aramean departure from five different perspectives, that of the narrator, the Arameans themselves, the lepers, the king of Israel, and the Israelite scouts. Against the narrator's omniscient perspective, the whole truth, we see the partial truths of the other limited perspectives and the efforts of the various actors to understand what has happened. The Arameans hear the supernatural sounds of mighty mercenary armies. As the enemy, they are wholly the victims of a divine ruse in which the reader can only delight. The lepers, concerned first about their stomachs, do not try to figure out what in fact became of the Arameans; they only fall on the food and valuables left behind. Yet once satisfied, their basic decency drives them to consider their fellow Israelites even though, as lepers, they have been shunned by them. The king of Israel assumes a ruse on the part of the Arameans, though ironically it is the Arameans themselves who have been fooled. He completely ignores the possibility that this news from the lowly lepers might have some link to Elisha's prophecy, that YHWH might be behind the Arameans' disappearance. His servant, on the other hand, takes a pragmatic approach, seeking full knowledge through observation: "let us send and find out" (v. 13). Finally, the scouts on the trail find the evidence proving that the lepers, and not the king, had correctly sized up the situation. Only after the scouts' confirmation has reached the king, does the narrator announce the fulfillment of the economic oracle spoken one day earlier by Elisha (v. 16).

A' Conclusion: Confirmation of Elisha's prophecy of the death of the aide (7:17-20)

The rest of the episode belabors the confirmation of the second oracle that Elisha had delivered to the king's aide who mocked the first oracle. With inverted word order, v. 17 breaks momentarily into narrated time to inform us that the king had put the aide in charge of the gate, just in time, perhaps, to be trampled by the people on their way out to plunder the Aramean camp. This death is then justified as a fulfillment of the oracle of the "man of God," and the confrontation scene between king and prophet is recapitulated (vv. 18-19). The words of v. 20, "and the people trampled him to death in the gate," repeat v. 17, thus forming an inclusio around the narrator's explanation. While the story of the lepers clearly led to the fulfillment of Elisha's first oracle, the slashing of prices on grain, the second oracle might have seemed unrelated to it. So vv. 17-20 fill in the gap by tying the trampling of the aide to Elisha's somewhat enigmatic oracle.

Chapter 11

RECALLING THE GREAT DEEDS OF ELISHA

2 Kings 8:1-6

This episode returns to the greatest of Elisha's miracles to provide a frame for the miracle stories as a whole. The anonymous king of Israel asks Gehazi to recite for him "all of the great deeds that Elisha did" (v. 4), as if the prophet were already dead and the miracles completed. Gehazi here functions as a disciple and an oral scribe expected to have compiled an account of his master's wonders and to be ready to deliver it on demand. Just as Gehazi gets to the tale of Elisha's revival of the dead boy, the boy himself suddenly appears on the scene along with his mother. Their presence confirms for the king the truth of Gehazi's testimony. Though Elisha appears in three more episodes, this tale rounds off the corpus of stories of Elisha as wonder-worker and so ends the main body of Elisha tales. Those later episodes disclose a rather different prophetic persona.

Here again time proves supple in the hand of the biblical narrator as he shifts among various pasts until he arrives at the present. Beginning with reverse word order to denote a past perfect, he recalls an interchange between Elisha and the Shunammite woman, here identified by means of a step further back into the past, as "the woman whose son he had revived." Elisha's words to her are also revived, appearing as direct speech (v. 1). This disclosure of further contact between Elisha and the woman surprises the reader for whom the woman's life after the revival of her son has been a blank. What became of her was of no interest until her return serves to confirm Elisha's authority in the presence of the king. Only now we discover that Elisha took an interest in the woman and, by sending her and her household away, sought to spare them the effects of the seven-year famine. Now, too, we discover that seven years have passed since that interchange, between her journey in v. 2 and her return in v. 3. The narrative present arrives at the end of v. 3, when the woman "went forth to cry out to the king about her house and her field." Her husband, absent emotionally in the earlier episode, here is absent altogether; his fate is a blank never filled. Ironically the woman who, in chap. 4, eschewed Elisha's offer to intercede with the king on her behalf, now resorts to this tactic herself.

Having traced the woman's story to the present, the narrator turns to the scene that she is about to enter. Switching to the participial form of the verb "speak" (v. 4) to denote "meanwhile," he introduces the dialogue between the king and Gehazi. The king's request is quoted, but Gehazi's answer appears in indirect discourse, the better to convey the shock of the woman's sudden appearance: "As he is recounting to the king how he revived the dead, . . . Look *(hinnēh)!* Here is the woman whose son he revived crying out to the king about her house and her field" (v. 5). The participles "recounting" and "crying" express the simultaneity of Gehazi's speech and the woman's complaint. Suddenly we see through Gehazi's eyes the surprise appearance in the present of the very woman whose past he is describing.

Now that Gehazi and the king have heard the woman's cry, announced by the narrator in v. 3, but not heard until v. 5, the forward movement of time can continue. Gehazi breaks out of indirect and into direct speech, proclaiming to the king, "this is the woman and this is her son whom Elisha revived" (v. 6). This is the fourth time the text has identified the son as the one revived by Elisha (cf. vv. 1, 5), underscoring the miraculous power of the departed prophet. The king, however, is represented questioning the woman, needing to hear her own account of the story before acceding to her request (v. 6). His order to restore to her all that was hers and to compensate her for her years of exile is magnanimous. On a strictly natural plane, it is an act of revivification as surely as Elisha's resuscitation of the boy. It shows a king transformed by the miracle of the man of God and willing to carry on his legacy.

Gehazi and the king have unusually positive images here. The king, who in the previous episode, wanted Elisha's head, now wants to hear of his mighty deeds. Most of all, the story seems designed to pay tribute to the authority of Elisha in his absence or after his death. It discloses his concern for the woman even after her son was revived and his continuing influence over her, for she obeyed his command to leave her land for seven years. It also shows his influence *in absentia* upon the king who asks for a recital of his miraculous deeds and pays tribute to the prophet through his treatment of the woman.

Part Two

REVOLUTIONS IN ARAM, ISRAEL, AND JUDAH

2 Kings 8:7–13:25

Chapter 12

ELISHA TRIGGERS A COUP IN ARAM:
HAZAEL TAKES POWER

2 Kings 8:7-15

Although the episode just concluded treats Elisha as if he were dead, in this tale he is very much alive. Here, and in the upcoming scene in 9:1-3, Elisha appears in a different role, not as wonder-worker but as fomenter of political revolutions. Until this point he has been represented as a supporter of the king of Israel, the usually unnamed Jehoram, son of Ahab. Even when, as in the battle against Moab, he denigrates Jehoram and praises the Judahite king Jehoshaphat, he still intervenes to save Israel's army and its king. Now, however, he issues oracles that promise to overturn the status quo, to overthrow the royal dynasties of both Aram and Israel.

Interestingly, it was not Elisha but Elijah who was ordered to anoint Hazael king of Aram and Jehu king of Israel (1 Kgs 19:15-18). Why does Elisha and not Elijah carry out these divinely ordained commandments? Nowhere does YHWH specifically transfer this responsibility to Elisha, nor does Elijah ever speak of the matter to his disciple. Historical critics explain this seeming contradiction by suggesting that each prophet became associated with these revolts in his own hagiographical tradition. Yet this explanation does not help make sense of the text as we have it. Does Elisha's fulfillment of tasks assigned to Elijah confirm the rejection of Elijah implicit in YHWH's choosing of Elisha (1 Kings 19) and his taking of Elijah in a fiery chariot?

In this penultimate appearance of Elisha, like that of Elijah (2 Kings 1), the prophet issues an oracle to a dying king. Recall that these two episodes are versions of a type-scene in which a mortally ill king sends a messenger to a prophet to find out what his fate will be. In several ways the tale at hand reverses the valences of the Elijah version. Whereas there Ahaziah, an Israelite king, sent to the foreign god Baal-zebub for an oracle, here Ben-hadad, the Aramean king, sends to Elisha the prophet of YHWH. And while Elijah predicts Ahaziah's death, Elisha promises Ben-hadad's recovery. Yet the relationship between the episodes is not one simply of reversal, but of development of the common type-scene in different ways. The chiastic structure of this episode focuses attention on the central dialogue between Hazael and Elisha, making the messenger here more important than the message.

A Introduction: sickness of Ben-hadad (v. 7)
  B Ben-hadad commissions Hazael (v. 8)
    C Hazael goes to Elisha (v. 9a)
      X Hazael and Elisha dialogue (vv. 9b-13)
    C' Hazael returns to Ben-hadad (v. 14)
  B' Ben-hadad receives Hazael (v. 14)
A' Conclusion: death of Ben-hadad (v. 15)

Like the Naaman tale, this one advertises the international reputation of Elisha. If Ahaziah intended to avoid Elijah, Ben-hadad sends directly to Elisha. If, in the previous episode, the king of Israel lauded Elisha, seemingly posthumously, here a foreign king—and a bitter enemy at that—further confirms for us Elisha's high status by taking the advice of those around him ("and it was told to him," v. 7) and commissioning Hazael to greet this "man of God" currently resident in Damascus. In fact, Elisha's unchallenged presence in Damascus suggests the wide sweep of his authority; earlier, by contrast, Naaman needed to travel to Israel to see him. Ben-hadad's rather general instructions to Hazael are expanded in the narrator's rendition of how Hazael carried them out, suggesting that the messenger uses his own initiative in the execution of his orders. Thus Ben-hadad tells him simply to take a gift, but Hazael takes "all the bounty of Damascus, forty camel-loads" (v. 9). And though Ben-hadad tells him "to greet the man of God," Hazael offers the obsequious greeting, "Your son, Ben-hadad king of Aram, sent me to you" (v. 9).

On the other hand, while Ben-hadad expressly instructs Hazael to inquire of YHWH through the prophet about his recovery, Hazael asks Elisha directly and does not ask him to inquire of YHWH. Thus Elisha's two-part answer to Hazael's first question, "Will I recover from this illness?" divides his own response from YHWH's. "Tell him, 'You shall surely recover,' but the LORD has shown me that he will surely die" (v. 10).

Technically, then, since Hazael did not ask Elisha for Y꜀ʜᴡʜ's response but only his own, Hazael is not deceptive when he transmits only the first half of Elisha's response to Ben-hadad (v. 14).

The second half of Elisha's answer is the first of two visions that Elisha relates to Hazael. Twice Elisha says, "the LORD has shown me" (vv. 10, 13) and reveals to Hazael the death of Ben-hadad and the accession to the throne of Hazael himself. Between these visions the narrator describes Elisha's facial contortion, perhaps an expression of pain, that issues in weeping. To Hazael's second question, "Why does my lord weep?" (v. 12), Elisha replies with a vivid description of the destruction that Hazael will wreak upon Israel. In poetic cadence he details the horrific fate of fortresses, men, children, and pregnant women. This oracle lies at the very center of the chiastic structure of the episode. It is the tragic outcome that Elisha is powerless to prevent even as he encounters the very agent of the destruction. To Hazael's astonished disavowal of the ability to do such a thing, Elisha appeals to a second vision, "the LORD has shown me you as king of Aram" (v. 13). Hazael offers no verbal reply to Elisha's final vision, but his killing of Ben-hadad makes him the agent of the enactment of the oracle. Commissioned by Ben-hadad, he becomes on his return the tool of Elisha; messenger has become murderer.

The episode ends with a regnal summary of four words—"he died, and Hazael reigned in his place"—thus including the Syrian succession in the divinely ordered regnal reigns and bringing them under the authority of the prophet. Indeed the next section, summarizing the succession in Judah, further incorporates the Hazael coup within the reigns of the kings.

Chapter 13

THE REIGNS OF JORAM AND AHAZIAH OF JUDAH

2 Kings 8:16-29

Following the detour to Damascus, two regnal summaries bring us up to date on events in Judah. The writer has used the long, twenty-five year reign of Jehoshaphat to focus attention on Elisha in the North without breaking the momentum to report regnal changes in the South. But since the coups that Elisha launches first in Aram and then in Israel spill over into Judah, the neglected Judahite history must be telescoped up to the narrative present.

Actually Jehoshaphat's accession is recorded way back in 1 Kgs 15:24. There too developments in Judah are suspended while the text reaches back in time to Nadab son of Jeroboam (1 Kgs 15:25) and forward through the reigns of Omri and Ahab. Only after Ahab's death (1 Kgs 22:37-40) in Jehoshaphat's eighteenth regnal year (1 Kgs 16:29; 22:41), does the writer finally offer a retrospective on Jehoshaphat's reign (1 Kgs 22:41-51). But then he returns immediately to the North where the reigns of Ahaziah and Jehoram serve as a backdrop for the last tales of Elijah and for the Elisha cycle. In fact, it has been so long without a mention of the Judahite king, that the narrator is compelled to remind us in 8:16 that Jehoshaphat's reign in Judah paralleled Jehoram's reign in Israel.

The description of the reign of Joram son of Jehoshaphat has two emphases. One is his link to the house of Ahab, still reigning in the North, through his unnamed wife, Ahab's daughter. Joram is the first king of Judah of whom it is said, "he walked in the way of the kings of Israel" (v. 18), and that behavior is blamed directly on his marriage. This marital connection foreshadows the upheaval in Judah soon to come. Since the Aramean coup has already occurred, we can expect the coup in Israel is soon to follow. And this link of Judah with the house of Israel foreshadows the spreading of revolution to Judah as well. Indeed, the narrator's editorial comment, "And the LORD did not consent to destroy Judah for the sake of David his servant," carries with it the connotation of "not yet." Why raise the specter of the destruction of Judah unless events are leading inevitably in that direction? In the meantime, the narrator's reference to YHWH's promise to Solomon (v. 19; cf. 1 Kgs 11:36) explains YHWH's restraint at the same time that it underscores divine control of events.

The other focus of the regnal summary is the rebellion of Edom, an ally against Moab during Jehoshaphat's reign (2 Kings 3), against Judahite suzerainty. Like Moab, Edom rebelled (*pāšaʿ*, vv. 20, 22), but here the rebellion is successful and permanent "until today" (v. 22). In contrast to the lengthy description of the allied action against Moab and the summoning of the prophetic word of Elisha, the rebellion of Edom is handled in one verse (v. 21) and supplemented with the seemingly contemporaneous rebellion of Libnah. In these successful revolts the seeds of Joram's unholy marriage with the house of Ahab would seem to have begun to germinate.

In the regnal summary of Ahaziah, Joram's son and successor, this king is doubly linked (vv. 25-29) to the sinful house of Ahab. He is the son of Athaliah, Omri's daughter (or granddaughter, if the text of v. 18 is read as written), and appears to be married to an unnamed Omride as well (v. 27). Hence, while the writer blames Ahaziah's father, Joram, for following the ways of the kings of Israel, he is more specific in his claim against Ahaziah who "walked in the way of the house of Ahab" (v. 27). By naming Athaliah as Ahaziah's mother (v. 26), the writer closes the gap opened when she is introduced as Joram's wife, but not named (v. 18). This attention to the Omride wife and mother signals subliminally her importance in what is to follow.

Instead of closing the curtain on Ahaziah's short one-year reign in Judah, as we might expect, and returning to a northern perspective, the writer moves into the future from within Ahaziah's regnal summary. He describes events preceding the tumultuous revolt of Jehu in Israel insofar as they intersect the life of Ahaziah. Thus the battle between Aram and Israel, in which King Jehoram of Israel is wounded, is described from Ahaziah's point of view: "He [Ahaziah] went with Jehoram, son of Ahab, to war . . ." (v. 28), and "Ahaziah son of Joram king of Judah was going down to see Jehoram son of Ahab in Jezreel, for he was sick" (v. 29). Even though Ahaziah is a bit player in the renewed conflict between Israel and Aram, his involvement with Joram will turn out to have a catastrophic impact upon him. In the meantime, the specification of Hazael as the aggressor confirms Elisha's prophecy that he will wreak havoc on Israel (v. 12). And with Hazael at war with Israel, can Jehu's coup, coupled with that of Hazael in YHWH's order to Elijah (1 Kgs 19:15-17), be far behind? With Ahaziah's file still open, the darkening clouds over Israel threaten to settle over Judah as well.

Chapter 14

THE REVOLUTION OF JEHU IN ISRAEL

2 Kings 9:1-10:36

The narrative of Jehu's overthrow of the Omride dynasty and destruction of the temple of Baal in Israel is the most gripping story in 2 Kings. A tale of conspiracy, deception, irony, and murder, it reopens the battle against apostasy begun by Elijah (1 Kings 18) but submerged during the Elisha narrative. Fulfilling the charge given to Elijah, Elisha triggers the anointing of Jehu who then executes a total revolution in Israel. By killing Ahaziah and his kinsmen, he provokes a coup in Judah as well. The narrative may be divided into two parallel sections.[1] In the first, Jehu assassinates in turn King Joram of Israel, King Ahaziah of Judah, and Jezebel, the queen mother of Israel. In the second section, he massacres the kinsmen of each king and the prophets of Baal, Jezebel's "kin." The narrative begins with the anointing of Jehu and YHWH's oracle supporting it, while it ends with a summary of his reign and YHWH's promise to him of a dynasty.

A Jehu is anointed king (9:1-15)
   B Jehu kills King Jehoram outside Jezreel (9:16-26)
   C Jehu kills King Ahaziah in Beth-haggan (9:27-29)
   D Jehu has Jezebel killed in Jezreel (9:30-37)

---

[1] This structure is suggested by Francisco O. Garcia-Treto, "The Fall of the House: A Carnivalesque Reading of 2 Kings 9 and 10," *Journal for the Study of the Old Testament* 46 (1990) 54.

B' Jehu massacres the house of Ahab in Jezreel (10:1-11)
C' Jehu massacres the kinsmen of King Ahaziah at Beth-eked
   (10:12-14)
D' Jehu massacres worshipers of Baal and destroys house of
   Baal in Samaria (10:15-28)
A' Summary of reign of Jehu (10:29-36)

A Jehu is anointed king (9:1-15)

With inverted subject-verb order, 9:1 shifts from Jehoram and Ahaziah in Jezreel to another story line. As Elisha provoked the overthrow of Ben-hadad through Hazael, now he engineers the coup against Jehoram by appointing a subordinate to anoint Jehu. His instructions to his disciple are quite specific, explaining what to bring, what to do, and what to say. His words emphasize the need to separate Jehu from his compatriots outside and to take him to an inside room where the anointing and commissioning are to take place. Then the disciple is told, "open the door and flee and don't wait around" (v. 3). This is a dangerous mission that must be accomplished in private, not public, space even though its ramifications will transform the public order.

The scene upon arrival in Ramoth-gilead, mediated through the disciple's eyes ("here are *[hinnēh]* soldiers sitting around," [v. 5]), is just as Elisha predicted, but the disciple uses his own ingenuity to separate Jehu from the rest. Hearing the man say that he has a message for the commander, Jehu questions which of the soldiers is meant. By speaking up, Jehu unintentionally reveals his identity, prompting the disciple to confirm that he, Jehu, is to be the recipient of the message.

The disciple adds two phrases to the formula of anointing (v. 6) articulated by Elisha that identify YHWH as the "god of Israel" and Israel as "the people of YHWH." These identifications begin to transform the delivery of Elisha's simple formula into a moment of high drama. The disciple then adds a long oracle of destruction over the house of Ahab (vv. 7-10) that stems not from Elisha but Elijah, when the latter prophesied to Ahab at Naboth's vineyard in Jezreel (1 Kgs 21:21-23). In the disciple's mouth, however, Jezebel has become the first object of vengeance because of her murder of the prophets. YHWH's wrath against her at the beginning and end of the prophecy prepares for the climactic role her death will play in Jehu's revolt. By summoning this prophetic voice from the past and reiterating it in the present, the disciple is used to articulate the larger divine scheme hidden in Elisha's curt oracle. With the background knowledge that Jehoram is recovering in Jezreel, the reader can sense that prophecy and place are about to converge. In the second half of the narrative, Jehu will indeed destroy both Ahab's descendants and Jezebel, whose gruesome murder in Jezreel the oracle predicts in detail. Indeed, one phrase added to the oracle, "none will bury her," adjusts the prophecy to the specific circumstances of Jezebel's death in unit D.

The secrecy surrounding Jehu's anointing does not last long. No sooner does the messenger flee than Jehu "went out" leaving the privacy and security of the inner room. Once outside, Jehu must face the questions of his comrades. Now they are identified as "servants of his master" to underscore their official loyalty to Joram and thereby the potential threat that they pose to Jehu should he reveal his "inside" information. In response to their curiosity about the *mĕšuggaʿ* (crazy man), Jehu first tries to dodge by agreeing with their evaluation of the disciple. The information that the disciple was seen as bizarre is reserved until after Jehu has heard his message. Does Jehu believe him or not? Only after the commanders call him a liar does Jehu answer truthfully, but even this is a partial truth. He omits the oracle entirely ("Thus and thus he said" [v. 12]) and transmits the formula of anointing as given by Elisha without the disciple's embellishments. That is, he tells them the bare minimum, and with oil presumably dripping off of his head, they might have guessed that anyway. Whatever doubts Jehu might have had are swept away by his comrades' immediate ("they hurried" [v. 13]) investiture ceremony and proclamation of him as king. The anointing was inside, but now outside on an upper landing, he is publicly acclaimed by his fellow commanders.

No sooner is he declared king than he hatches a conspiracy against Jehoram (v. 14a). An aside (vv. 14b-15a), set off in the Hebrew as a separate paragraph, recalls that Jehoram is recuperating in Jezreel from the wounds suffered in the battle with the Arameans while the troops are at Ramot Gilead. Interrupting Jehu's conversation with his comrades, this information underscores the timeliness of Jehu's conspiracy. If there were ever a good moment to eliminate the king, it is now when he is ailing and apart from his troops. In order to make a sneak attack Jehu then demands silence from his comrades (v. 15b).

B Jehu kills King Joram outside Jezreel (9:16-26)

The second section begins with movement, Jehu's ride to Jezreel. There, we are reminded yet again, Jehoram is "lying down" and Ahaziah is visiting—sitting ducks for Jehu's aggression. Now through the eyes of a lookout on a tower in Jezreel we see Jehu's approach to the city (v. 17). Though the narrator reports from an omniscient perspective what the lookout sees, for the lookout the picture only gradually comes into focus. Joram's sending and Jehu's commandeering of two successive hapless horsemen draw attention to the unknown identity of the man who approaches. Though the reader is privileged to hear Jehu's spurning of the horsemen's question, "Is all well?" the lookout can only report their capture. Finally the man's "crazy" driving style as he draws closer identifies him as Jehu to the lookout, who duly reports his observation to Jehoram. Interestingly the same Hebrew word meaning "crazy" that Jehu's comrades associated with the prophetic disciple who anointed him is here associated with Jehu himself.

Jehoram is represented as needing no other information before hitching up and riding out, along with Ahaziah, to meet Jehu (v. 21). Noting that each king is in his own chariot, the narrator prepares for their separate but identical fates. Without comment, he also notes that they confront each other at Naboth's vineyard, the site where the oracle delivered to Jehu was originally pronounced by Elijah. Piece by piece the writer constructs the conditions for the fulfillment of the prophecy. The last piece of the puzzle is Jezebel, recalled in the oracle and now evoked specifically by Jehu in response to Jehoram's own repetition of the question that the horsemen had previously asked Jehu: "Is all well, Jehu?" Jehu replies by naming "Jezebel your mother" as the cause of the apostasy that plagues Israel (v. 22). Again Jehoram is represented taking immediate action, now fleeing from Jehu, and warning Ahaziah as well. Switching to inverted subject-verb order (v. 23), the narrator expresses the simultaneity of Jehoram's flight and Jehu's taking aim at him with his bow. With relish he reports in forensic style the exact path of the arrow as it brings Jehoram down in his chariot (v. 24).

Following the assassination of Jehoram, Jehu discloses the surprising information that he and Bidkar heard the original pronouncement of the oracle against Ahab to avenge the death of Naboth (cf. 1 Kgs 21:20-24). This brief flashback links Jehu to Ahab directly and sheds new light on Jehu's reaction to his anointing by the *mĕšuggaʿ*. If he accepted the disciple's oracle without question, that was, we now may assume, because he had heard it before. His self-confident conspiracy was fueled by the doubled divine word. Now he even gives his own version of that word, expanding it even beyond what the disciple had said by claiming divine vengeance not only for Naboth but also for his sons. He thus justifies the slaying of the son of Ahab as recompense for the murder of the sons of Naboth. He frames his pronouncement with the order to Bidkar to throw Joram into the field of Naboth, fulfilling prophecy, and prophet-like he piously so declares the prophecy fulfilled. Although Jehu first appears in the narrative in this chapter when anointed by the young prophet, his own recollections depict him, Forrest Gump-like, as participant in a crucial moment in earlier history. Jehu's flashback further reinforces the divine control over history and the providential presence of the future revolutionary at Naboth's field then and now.

C Jehu kills King Ahaziah in Beth-haggan (9:27-29)

Again inverted word order establishes simultaneity: of Joram's murder and Ahaziah's flight: "When Ahaziah, king of Judah saw, he fled" (v. 27). Jehu's single utterance in this scene, "Him too shoot!," the direct object pointedly in first position, sets into motion an assassination that oversteps the divine orders in the oracle given to him. In fact, the Hebrew lacks the verb ("and they shot him") that would indicate compliance with the order, letting Jehu's words alone, as it were, strike him down.[2] The responsibility for this murder and the political turmoil in Judah resulting from it is thus made to rest on Jehu alone. Already, then, the positive evaluation of Jehu implied in his execution of the divine initiative against the house of Ahab is negatively colored by his unauthorized extension of the revolution to Judah. Indeed, the immediate attention to the proper conveyance of Ahaziah to Jerusalem and burial in the city of David "with his fathers" (v. 28), in contrast to the unceremonious dumping of Joram in Naboth's field, suggests the writer's sympathy for a Davidide done in.

D Jehu has Jezebel killed in Jezreel (9:30-37)

The two monarchs disposed of, Jehu goes after Jezebel who is identified twice in this narrative, by the prophet and by Jehu himself, as the source of the evil which the kings sponsored. As Jehu rides to Jezreel, we see Jezebel primping in her boudoir, preparing for his arrival. Her actions, denoted by a series of parallel verbs, mark time as Jehu journeys toward her. She paints, pretties, and peers out her window. From her perspective we see Jehu enter the gate. She greets him (v. 31) with

---

[2] This omission is likely due to haplography (the inadvertent writing of a word once when it should have been repeated) in the manuscript tradition. Here the text omits "and they shot him" immediately after the imperative "shoot!"

the same initial word used by the lookouts and by Joram: *hašālôm?* ("Is all well?"). But her greeting immediately turns bitter when she labels him a Zimri, the name of another army officer who several generations earlier had committed treason by slaying King Elah and the rest of the Baasha clan (1 Kgs 16:9-13). Some critics have suggested that both eye-painting and hair-arranging were preparations for love-making and that Jezebel intended to seduce Jehu. The word *zimrî* they take as a common noun meaning "hero."[3] But the parallel between Jehu's trea-son and Zimri's is too strong to be ignored and the epithet "murderer of his master" is hardly designed to flame Jehu's desire. Jezebel adorns herself because in her own eyes she is still the queen mother, the power behind the throne. From that regal position, looking down from her window, she challenges the authority of the traitor Jehu.

The narrator draws out the dramatic effect of Jezebel's position at the window overlooking Jehu. Only after Jehu hears her taunting words does he "lift his face to the window" (v. 32). And when two or three eunuchs align themselves with him, he issues a one-word order just as he did when he ordered Ahaziah slain: "Throw her down!" Similar to that scene as well is the detailed and gory picture of the vic-tim's death, here featuring splattering blood and trampling horses (v. 33). From safety inside to death outside, from the heights to the depths, this movement in the episode expresses the transformation of the po-litical order by the transgression of physical boundaries.[4] Recall as well the potential danger that the young prophet and Jehu faced when they left the inner room and the actual danger that Jehoram and Ahaziah met when they "went out" from Jezreel.

Jehu's cold resoluteness is expressed in his reaction to Jezebel's death: "He went (inside), he ate, and he drank" (v. 34). While her blood is splat-tering on the wall, (an allusion to the idiom for the males of the house of Ahab, "pissers against the wall" [9:8][5]), Jehu is filling his stomach. As his horses trample Jezebel, he drinks in her house. When he does order her burial, it is with heavy irony, for he calls her both "an accursed thing" and "a king's daughter." The irony deepens when she cannot be found, and only the skull, feet, and hands remain (v. 35); the body of Jezebel has been devoured while Jehu was himself devouring her food in her house.

The scene ends with Jehu again proclaiming the fulfillment of prophecy, this time citing Elijah the Tishbite by name as the spokes-

---

[3] See the discussion of Burke O. Long, *2 Kings*. The Forms of the Old Testament Literature, vol. X (Grand Rapids: Eerdmans, 1991) 129.

[4] Garcia-Treto, "Fall," 47–62.

[5] Ibid., 58.

man of the oracle. As the narrative began with the young prophet's delivery of this oracle to Jehu and proceeded with Jehu's reference to it to justify the disposal of Jehoram's corpse in Naboth's field, now it ends with an invocation of the prophet who originally uttered the oracle. Jehu is declaring himself the agent of providence in bringing about the events predicted long ago by Elijah. Yet, as earlier (v. 26), Jehu expands Elijah's oracle. The prediction that Jezebel's corpse will be like dung and that no one will be able to recognize her is not part of Elijah's original prophecy (1 Kgs 21:23). If her blood is splattered against the wall like urine and her body turned into dung, Jezebel has become pure waste. Does this suggest that Jehu is opportunistically making the prophecy fit the facts? Or as a witness to Elijah's delivery of the oracle, is he simply remembering what was not recorded earlier? In either case he appears as an authoritative interpreter of prophecy who has finally ended the long reign of Jezebel. With the reigning members of the house of Ahab now dead, he turns to their heirs.

B' Jehu massacres the house of Ahab in Jezreel (10:1-11)

The narrative now swings from Jezebel to Ahab, from the mother of all evil to the father who sponsored it. Jehu's next move is to eliminate the house of Ahab, whose name is the first word in this episode. The house of Ahab is epitomized in the number of seventy descendants, a full house, so to speak, like those of Jacob (Exod 1:5) and Gideon (Jud 8:30). In a series of two letters Jehu's strategy is revealed, to the reader at the same time as to their addressees.

First, he challenges the "princes of Jezreel, the elders, and the guardians (of the descendants) of Ahab" (v. 1) to appoint a king from among Ahab's sons to fight it out with Jehu. Leading with and repeating the word "with you," he stresses that his recipients have all the power: the descendants of Ahab, the chariots, horses, fortified city, and weapons. Thus painting himself as the underdog, he urges them to choose "the best *(haṭṭôb)* and the most appropriate" of Ahab's sons for "his father's" throne. His words are tinged with irony, for what would qualify one as "the best"? The easiest for Jehu to slaughter? Only after he bids them to choose a leader does he conclude by challenging them to battle. He tells them to "look for" *(ûrĕ²îtem)* an heir but they react, in a play on words, by "fearing" *(wayyir²û,* v. 4), and fearing very greatly. To themselves they admit their fear to stand against the assassin of two kings. To Jehu they express their obsequiousness and make him king by default, ceding to him the right to do "what is best" *(haṭṭôb,* v. 5). In essence they have offered themselves as covenant partners: "Your servants we are, and all that you say, we will do" (v. 5).

Having thus sworn allegiance to Jehu, they are in no position to argue when he demands, in somewhat ambiguous language, the heads of those who remain of the house of Ahab. Jehu's second letter echoes the covenant language of the officials' reply: "If you are with me and to my voice you are listening . . ." (v. 6). Slaughter will be the price of covenant loyalty. The slaughter is made all the more horrendous by the information in v. 6 that the very city officials *(gĕdolê hāʿîr)* who had raised *(mĕgadlîm)* them now became their murderers. Though the first letter was sent to a variety of named officials in Samaria, the second one is received by the child-raisers alone. Now the narrator reveals none of their thoughts, only reports their action: they "slaughter," "put" heads in baskets, and "send," distancing themselves from their crime as well as from Jehu (v. 7).

But if the town notables hoped to escape the murderous usurper by offering Ahab's descendants to him, they were wrong. Instead Jehu turns the tables by using the display of bloody heads at the city gate to justify the slaughter of whoever remained of the house of Ahab in Jezreel. Before the horrific exhibit, reminiscent of the terrorist practices of some neo-Assyrian kings, Jehu addresses "all the people" of Jezreel.[6] While accepting blame for the assassination of the king, he deceptively proclaims his innocence in the deaths of the sons. The reader, but not Jehu's audience, knows of the correspondence that provoked the slaughter of the seventy. Jehu implicitly spreads the responsibility over the assembled ("Are you so righteous?"), but then, for good measure, evokes divine causation as well, citing the fulfillment of Elijah's prophecy of the destruction of the house of Ahab (v. 10). And to complete the work, Jehu finally kills whoever remains of the house of Ahab in Jezreel as well as those officials who supported it.

In this episode the narrator refrains from judging Jehu directly, but his actions and words project a figure increasingly taken up by his own historical role. While in the assassination of Jehoram, Jehu simply enacted the oracle given to him, in the murder of Jezebel he displays both viciousness, and in his scatological interpretation of her remains, sick perversity. Furthermore, the writer's spotlight on Jehu's underhanded strategy with the guardians of Ahab's descendants and his terroristic use of their severed heads illuminates a man who relishes the vengeance he feels called upon to wreak. And his extension of the

---

[6] Mordechai Cogan and Hayim Tadmor, *II Kings,* Anchor Bible 11 (Garden City, NY: Doubleday, 1988) 113.

bloodbath beyond the house of Ahab to "officials, intimates, and priests" (v. 11) takes his actions beyond even his own elaborations of Elijah's prophecy.

C' Jehu massacres the kinsmen of Ahaziah at Beth-eked (10:12-14)

Corresponding to the assassination of King Ahaziah in unit C, this short scene depicts Jehu's slaughter of Ahaziah's kinsmen who, unluckily, find themselves in his path as he approaches Samaria. They present themselves to Jehu honestly, identifying themselves as "kinsmen of Ahaziah" just as the narrator has identified them (v. 13). At the same time they announce that they are on a journey of peace to the descendants of Jehoram and Jezebel. Since they specify the descendants, they would seem to know that both the king and queen mother are dead and, if so, who killed them. But Jehu does not identify himself, so it is not clear if they recognize him or know that he has already slaughtered the very people whom they are on their way to visit. What is clear is Jehu's brutal reaction. Though they stress their peaceful intentions (*lišlôm*, v. 13), he orders that they be taken alive and then slaughtered. The number forty-two echoes the number of boys mauled by the bears summoned by Elisha, in other words, a large round number. As in the previous scene, the narrator confirms that no one survives the slaughter. Interestingly the place names where both Ahaziah and his kinsmen encounter Jehu are formed with the word *bêt* (house)—Beth-haggan and Beth-eked—an echo, perhaps, of the "house" of Ahab that Jehu is in the process of destroying.

D' Jehu massacres worshipers of Baal and destroys the house of Baal in Samaria (10:15-28)

A second chance meeting on the way to Samaria results not in murder but alliance. After securing Jehonadab ben Rekhev's loyalty and grasping his hand, Jehu welcomes him into his chariot. Word-play reinforces the alliance on the sound level, for Jehonadab's patronymic, *rekeb*, sounds in the words for bless (*wayĕbārkēhû*, v. 15), make ride (*wayyarkibû*, v. 16), and chariot (*hammerkābāh*, v. 15; *bĕrikbô*, v. 16). It is as if Jehonadab's presence augments the power of the chariot. Jehu's profession of zeal for YHWH is expressed by the narrator in the report of his slaughter of whoever still survived of Ahab's house in Samaria.

This scene, like the two previous ones, ends with the confirmation of total annihilation. Here too the prophecy of Elijah is invoked, this time by the narrator. This scene balances that in 9:25-26 in which Jehu calls upon another ally, Bidkar, with whom he recalls another chariot ride.

No sooner are the remnants of the house of Ahab eliminated than Jehu turns his attention to the worshipers of Baal and to the house of Baal. As in Jezreel, he addresses in Samaria "all the people" and again speaks deceptively as the narrator notes in a rare evaluative intrusion (v. 19b). Like Elijah at Mount Carmel, Jehu aims to destroy Baal worship—this the narrator announces—but to the people he poses as Baal's champion, more pious than the infamous Ahab. Leading with the compound direct object for emphasis ("all the prophets of Baal, all his worshipers, and all his priests"), Jehu calls upon the people to gather these Baal devotees together for a sacrifice to Baal and threatens death to anyone who does not show up. Only in retrospect can we see the irony of his words, for the assembled themselves become the sacrifice, and only those missing could possibly escape. For the moment the narrator's intrusion confirms Jehu's guile even if we cannot yet see his plan.

The episode continues to present Jehu's public face and conceal his true intentions. Inside the house of Baal, Jehu's pledge to outdo Ahab proceeds apace. The sanctuary is filled "mouth to mouth" (v. 21) with Baal worshipers for whom Jehu orders vestments to be brought. As their patron Jezebel adorned herself to meet Jehu, so the worshipers are made to dress up for the occasion. Along with Jehonadab, to whom Jehu had promised to show his zeal for YHWH, he orders that all YHWH worshipers leave, and those remaining inside offer "sacrifices and burnt offerings." Only after the sacrifice inside the temple is well underway is the scene outside revealed—to the reader but not to the participants inside. Thus as the festivities proceed inside the house, the narrator discloses that the house has been surrounded by Jehu's men, instructed by Jehu to let no one escape (v. 24). This subtle time shift to the immediate past is signaled by inverted word order ("Jehu positioned outside," v. 24b). Only in v. 25 do outside and inside converge when Jehu orders his men to attack the worshipers. Only now as it is enacted is his plan fully revealed. In their sacred garments the worshipers go to their deaths silently, their surprised reaction to Jehu's double-cross left to the imagination.

The worshipers disposed of, or rather, left lying unburied[7] like Jezebel, Jehu's men turn to the "house of Baal" itself. Though the Hebrew is not altogether clear, the focus is on the burning of the sacred

---

[7] See Cogan and Tadmor, *II Kings,* 116.

pillars of the house and, perhaps, the altar of Baal as well. Finally the house itself is torn down and turned into either a latrine or simply a dung heap. In either case, its link with excrement ties it to the remains of Jezebel, likened to dung on the ground (9:37). The chronological bridge to the present, "until today," gives an etiological twist to the tale as it sounds the final death knoll on Baal worship in Israel. The dung heap in Samaria in the writer's day, on what was believed to be the site of Baal's temple, symbolizes for him the eradication of Baal worship.

A' Summary of the reign of Jehu (10:29-36)

From the account of the destruction of Baal's worshipers and temple the text moves directly to the conclusion of Jehu's reign. Nothing but his initiating acts in Jezreel and Samaria are dramatized; in but a few lines the rest of his reign is summarized. Clearly, Jehu's claim to fame rests in the elimination of the house of Ahab and the extirpation of Baal worship, including the "house of Baal." The other events of his reign merit only the briefest mention and further problematize the already problematic *modus operandi* of this fiery revolutionary.

No sooner has Jehu been credited with eradicating Baal from Israel than he is criticized for not also eliminating the golden calves at Beth-el and Dan; thus, although he has eliminated the sins of the house of Ahab, he is criticized for falling into the sinful pattern of Jeroboam, the writer's arch-villain (v. 29). And no sooner has the narrator leveled this critique than the voice of YHWH is interjected directly into the narration, praising Jehu for having "successfully done the right thing in my eyes according to everything that was in my heart to the house of Ahab" (v. 30). This unqualified praise is followed by YHWH's promise of a four-generation dynasty. Yet in the next verse (v. 31) the narrator takes up his critique again, sandwiching YHWH's praise in a sea of negativity. By thus checking (hedging?) divine plaudits with his own appraisal, the writer is able to account both for the continuation of Jehu's line and the reduction of his territory (v. 32). Indeed both divine and human causation (the perennial challenge by Hazael) are invoked to explain the loss of land east of the Jordan. But in his last statement on Jehu, the narrator does modify the summary formula to include mention of "all of his heroism" (v. 34), thus offering a final one-word tribute to the king.

This closing ambivalence about the character of Jehu well reflects the entire presentation. On the one hand, he is charged by Elisha's messenger with destroying the house of Ahab and is praised for doing so. On the other hand, he goes beyond the call of duty in his vehemence and deviousness. He takes advantage of Jehoram's medical condition, presses the guardians of Ahab's descendants to kill their wards, and gratuitously slaughters the peaceable kin of Ahaziah. He is shown in constant movement and bloody slaughters. To every question about peace—from his comrades, Jehoram, Jezebel—he responds with war. Furthermore, as one critic puts it, he too conveniently has a divine oracle at hand whenever he needs one.[8] In fact, his repeated elaborations of Elijah's oracle get no confirmation from the narrator, raising further questions about his integrity. Yet for all of his *šiggāʿôn* ("madness," 9:20), he accomplishes what had been left undone since Elijah's days: the wiping out of Baalism and its sponsors in Israel. While this laudable end is thus praised, Jehu's methods are severely criticized.

---

[8] George Savran, "1 and 2 Kings," *The Literary Guide to the Bible,* ed. Robert Alter and Frank Kermode (Cambridge: Harvard, 1987) 153.

Chapter 15

JEHOIADA ENGINEERS THE OVERTHROW OF ATHALIAH AND THE ACCESSION OF JEHOASH IN JUDAH

2 Kings 11:1-20

Having leaped forward twenty-eight years to close Jehu's reign, the writer doubles back to pick up the action in Judah which would have been concurrent with Jehu's coup. Concurrence is indicated by the use of an inverse word order that conveys a past perfect sense: "When Athaliah, mother of Ahaziah had seen that her son was dead . . ." Previously, Athaliah has been simply the name of the queen mother (8:26), though as the daughter of Omri, she was automatically suspect. But now, in one verse, she becomes the counterpart in Judah to Jezebel, her infamous sister-in-law in Israel. She becomes the epitome of wickedness, the cause of the destruction of all the "seed of the royal house." Why does she do it? Is it because she thinks that if her son cannot rule, no other Davidide may rule either? Is it because, as the sole surviving member of the house of Ahab, she seeks to preserve her dynasty in Judah? She is given neither thought nor voice to express herself. Unlike Jehu's massacres in Israel, hers receive neither explanation nor dramatization. In fact, her action is expressed in a formal and sanitized way—not as murder or slaughter but as destruction: "she made to perish all the seed of the royal house" (v. 1). Even though she does no more than what Jehu had done in Israel, liquidation of the royal house, she is not viewed ambivalently. Rather, her wickedness is expressed backhandedly in the detail given to the plot to overthrow her.

The second verse sets Ahaziah's sister as the savior of Ahaziah's baby son against Ahaziah's mother, Athaliah. Unbeknownst to Athaliah, Jehosheba, identified as daughter and sister, appears to snatch her nephew from the jaws of death "from the midst of" *(mittôk)* the king's descendants as they were being slain. Like baby Moses, saved by Pharaoh's daughter and his own sister from the edict of Pharaoh, baby Jehoash is rescued by one woman and nursed by another (cf. Exod 2:5-7). But here the drama pits one woman against another: a mother who slaughters children against an aunt who saves her nephew. In an interscenic summary (v. 3) parallel participial clauses align the hiding of Jehoash with the reigning of Athaliah. The secret king is concealed within, while the public queen reigns "over the land"; six years pass in a verse.

The narrative moves directly to the seventh year, in which the reversal of outside and inside are engineered. The hiding king is brought out into the light and the reigning queen is taken inside and put to death. The instigator of the restoration is Jehoiada who appears without introduction giving orders to royal guards who obey him without question. Though we learn elsewhere (2 Chr 22:11) that he is married to Jehosheba, that information is not given here. Though his position in the temple would indicate that he is a priest, even that is not confirmed until verse 9. Jehoiada acts swiftly to secure the loyalty of the palace guard by "cutting a covenant" and extracting an unspecified oath from them in the "house of the LORD" (v. 4). Like Jehu who uses the guard to entrap the followers of Baal, Jehoiada will employ the palace guard to capture Athaliah. Implicit is the contrast between the palace where Athaliah rules and the "house of the LORD" where Jehoiada holds sway. Only after securing the loyalty of the troops does Jehoiada show them young Jehoash.

Next, in great detail (vv. 5-8), Jehoiada spells out to the guard the security arrangements to be implemented for the coronation of the new king. All the plans are put into his mouth as direct address, conveying his control over a presumably very dangerous situation. And no sooner are the words out of his mouth than the narrator confirms that they did "everything that Jehoiada the priest commanded" (v. 9). No sudden, bloody coup this. For seven years Jehoiada had been biding his time, and now everything is to proceed like clockwork. By dividing the on-duty guard into thirds around the palace, Jehoiada makes sure that Athaliah cannot escape. And by drafting the off-duty guard to protect Jehoash in the temple, he covers the territory of both "houses." In addition, he orders the forces to be on highest alert, weapons at hand (vv. 8, 11), ready to kill anyone who threatens the plan (v. 8).

In verses 9-11 the narrator augments our sense of Jehoiada's control by repeating the arrangements in their execution and adding information that underscores the legitimacy of Jehoiada's plan. In verse 9 Jehoiada is twice (and for the first time!) identified as "the priest." To him, the narrator explains, the officers presented their troops before deploying them. He thus functions as commander-in-chief, a priest who is simultaneously a military leader. Jehoiada gives the officers weapons that belonged to King David himself, bolstering the troops with the legitimacy of the house of David as they face the pretender now on the throne.

With the troops in place, Jehoiada brings "the king's son" outside for the first time. Since the beginning of the narration of the seventh year, the narrator has never referred to him by name but only by title: the king or the king's son. Thus even before his enthronement he was really already the king. Now, in an official coronation ceremony he is invested with the symbols of power, "the crown and the ʿēdût," interpreted variously as "jewels" or "testimony," of office. In rapid succession the assembled acclaim him king, anoint him, applaud, and declare, "Long live the king." These verbs of investiture come quickly and without interruption. Jehoiada's plan comes off without a hitch—so far!

With the coronation complete, the scene shifts to Athaliah at the palace. While Jehoiada's plans were executed in secret, once the coronation goes public she is drawn into the action. The narrator first describes what she hears: the voices of acclamation carry to the palace and she comes to the house of YHWH immediately. The scene there is then described from her perspective opening with *hinnēh* ("behold"): "the king standing next to the pillar, as ordained, and the princes and the trumpets for the king and all the people of the land happy and blowing the trumpets" (v. 14). Before she reacts her eyes take it all in, and we see her seeing. She is permitted by Jehoiada and the narrator to come unmolested to the scene of her downfall. Rather than simply describe the crowd's rejoicing over the new king, the writer heightens the dramatic effect by displaying the scene through Athaliah's ears and eyes. She might have been captured on her way from palace to temple, but instead she is allowed to witness the enactment of her worst nightmare.

Having heard and seen, Athaliah reacts (v. 14b). With two rhyming verbs she tears *(wattiqraʿ)* her clothes and she cries out *(wattiqrāʾ)*. And her cry, though only one word twice repeated—"Conspiracy! *(qešer)*"—reveals her full realization of what has happened in the temple while she ruled the land. A form of this word appeared earlier in the narrator's preview of Jehu's plot against Jehoram (9:14). Its repetition here suggests a link between this conspiracy and the one which launched Jehu, and by extension Athaliah, into power. Seven years later a counterplot restores the proper heir to the throne of Judah, canceling Athaliah's usurpation.

Only after Athaliah has recognized the significance of what has happened does Jehoiada order the guard to remove her and her supporters. Although the exact location referred to in the Hebrew is unclear, Jehoiada's follow-up words—"Let her not be put to death in the house of the LORD" (v. 15)—show his insistence on removing her from the temple precinct. Indeed, when he utters those words he is identified not by name but by title: "for the priest said (or thought)." Jehoiada's priestly concern that her blood not profane the house of YHWH directs him to return her to the palace where she ruled and where she shall die. In fact, she is brought into the palace area through the horses' entrance, recalling the death by trampling horses of her sister-in-law, Jezebel. Unlike Jehu's rampage against the house of Ahab and Athaliah's own massacre of her husband's descendants, Jehoiada restores the house of David by a single execution. In contrast to Jehu and Athaliah, Jehoiada has scruples implicitly attributed to his priestly office.

In the final movement of the royal restoration, the way is prepared for the return of the legitimate Davidide to the palace. The first order of business is the making of a covenant. Jehoiada's first action was the "cutting" of a covenant with the officers of the guard by means of which he secured their loyalty for the coming coup. Now with Athaliah dead he turns to the people as a whole with a covenant of rededication, implicating YHWH, king, and people. The reign of Athaliah is thus viewed as an interruption of the relationship that had existed before her usurpation. To cancel that interregnum and to begin again requires a new covenant. As a sign of their loyalty, "all the people of the land" then tear down Baal's temple, smash its sancta, and slay its priest (v. 18). (The term "people of the land" [cf. v. 14] most likely refers to an elite social group, probably wealthy, whose loyalty was necessary to secure the new regime.) As in the North, both political and religious illegitimate regimes are eliminated. The scene ends, as in grand opera, with all of the principal actors (Jehoiada, the chiefs of the guard) and the chorus ("all the people of the land") leading the boy king to his throne. Emphasized is the movement from the "house of the LORD" to the "house of the king." The legitimate and the sacred extends its reach into what had been profaned by Athaliah and Baal. "And he sat on the throne of the kings" (v. 19b) continuing the tradition of his forefathers.

The final verse of narration turns to the consequences of the tumultuous event, the return of order and balance. Ironically, though "all the people of the land" rejoice, the city itself is calm. This is not the brutal revolution that occurred in Israel, rather a restoration of equilibrium to a people who wanted it. Note that no one supported Athaliah. She stood alone observing the acclamation of the new king and alone was put to death. Indeed, lest we had forgotten her fate, a coda (v. 20b) reminds us. The contrast between the bloody, horrific massacres of Jehu and the swift, orderly coup of Jehoiada could not be sharper.

Chapter 16

THE ACHIEVEMENT AND FAILURE
OF KING JEHOASH

2 Kings 12:1-22

A mixed record (12:1-4)

The account of the reign of King Jehoash begins with the first part of a proper regnal summary, synchronizing the year of the succession of Jehoash with the seventh year of Jehu of Israel. Athaliah had received no such respect. The illegitimacy of her reign is expressed by the absence of a regnal summary. Her regime is outside the file of any king and she is given no file of her own. By coordinating Jehoash but not Athaliah to Jehu's reign, it is as if she never existed.

Set off in the Hebrew as a separate paragraph before the regnal summary proper and thus commanding special attention is a noun clause giving the age of Jehoash when he ascended the throne (12:1). Clearly at age seven he was king only *de jure*, so it is no surprise that he did what Jehoiada the priest told him to do (v. 3). It is also no surprise that, given the influence of his priestly mentor, the sole project dramatized during his long forty-year reign is the temple repair affair. Yet before that story and after praising Jehoash's fidelity to YHWH, the narrator criticizes his inertia with regard to the shrines and *bamôt*, the local places of worship not connected with the Jerusalem temple. This Deuteronomistic critique of Judahite kings, repeated here, casts a shadow over the otherwise happy restoration and points uneasily toward a future resolution. For now, though, the writer turns to Jehoash's repairs of the temple.

Jehoash repairs the Temple (12:5-17)

His first reported act is a command to the priests to create a building fund for the repair of "breaches *(bedeq).*" The source of revenue is to be twofold. First, the priests are to collect pledges from people who have vowed to contribute their own personal value to the Temple. Leviticus 27:1-8 establishes equivalents in silver by age and gender for votary offerings, and something like this scale must be operating in Jehoash's order. Second, the priests are to collect voluntary donations. Emphasized in this plan is the individual responsibility of the priests both to receive the money ("each from his benefactor," v. 6) and to make the necessary repairs. That the writer puts this emphasis in Jehoash's mouth alerts us to the possibility of abuse of priestly power, an abuse that next comes into play.

At what point in his reign Jehoash issued this order is not specified, but in his twenty-third regnal year no repairs had yet been made. Why is this year, but not the year of the order, specified? How long had the priests been pocketing the silver? Had they ignored Jehoash because of his youth? Though the text is silent on these issues, it makes clear that at age thirty, Jehoash takes charge and addresses not only the priests but also his mentor, Jehoiada, with a stern question and new command. To his challenge (v. 8) the priests are silent, pleading no contest to his implied charge of corruption. To his new order forbidding them from taking the money directly and charging them to turn it over for repairs, the narrator reports that the priests consent, as if they are too embarrassed to speak for themselves (v. 9).

Interestingly, the text highlights the method for assuring that the money brought in to the temple be used for repairs and that it not find its way into the pockets of the priests. First, Jehoiada gets into the act, fashioning a collection box out of a chest and placing it in the proper spot for worshipers entering the temple. Then, shifting to the participle *běbôʾ* ("when they would come," v. 10b), the narrator describes the recurring pattern of deposit, collection, counting, and delivery of the money. Now the priests are not left to their own devices; others are responsible for overseeing the money at each stage. Priestly guards watch over the collection box, while the king's scribe and high priest handle the counting of the silver and then hand it over to the contractors, who in turn pay the tradesmen.

While one might argue that the more hands that touch the cash, the more chances for graft, the clear message here is that the distinct responsibilities provide a system of checks to assure honesty. Lest there be any doubt, we are assured that the overseers "acted in good faith" (v. 16). This assurance implicitly casts a negative judgment on the priests who had offered no defense when Jehoash upbraided them. Nor does the narrator defend them. The thrust of this account is to show Jehoash as not simply a creature of the priest Jehoiada who put him into power but as a decisive leader who reins in the priestly establishment. It also praises the non-priestly contractors for their honesty. As a final note, the narrator assures us that the priests are also dealt with fairly, for they continue to receive the proceeds brought in for guilt and sin offerings (v. 17). It seems appropriate that Jehoash, raised and hidden in the temple during his formative years, would care deeply about its upkeep and that the writer would highlight this aspect of his reign.

Jehoash pays tribute to Hazael of Aram (12:18-19)

With only the loosest of transitions ("then"), the writer turns from Jehoash's major achievement to his worst disaster when King Hazael of Aram reappears. Reported to have attacked Israel at the very end of the account of the reign of Jehu, now Hazael threatens Jerusalem. Just as after the story of the elimination of the house of Ahab and the Baalists from the North, Israel's borders are threatened, so too here. After the overthrow of Athaliah and the re-establishment of the Davidic monarchy, the writer widens his horizon to report Hazael's advance on Jerusalem. In both cases the information about Hazael's incursions is reserved until after equilibrium has been restored. The effect is to upset the newly achieved balance and throw Judah's future once more into doubt. Elisha's prediction of Hazael's bloody future (8:12) continues to bear fruit.

Jehoash, whose life work has been telescoped into his temple repair, responds to Hazael's incursion by raiding the temple for tribute. His subservience to Hazael is expressed by specifying the extent of his gift: "all the sancta that had been sanctified" by his three predecessors and himself and "the sancta and all the gold" from both the temple and palace treasuries (v. 9). He holds nothing back in his effort to save the city even if it means losing everything of value.

An ignominious end (12:20-22)

The narrator issues no direct evaluation of Jehoash's payment of tribute though he does not defend his action either. Yet the conspiracy against him by his courtiers and his assassination (v. 21) clearly represent major dissatisfaction with his policies. Nor are his assassins criticized; their deed is merely reported and their names given. It is all quite matter-of-fact. So the reign of Jehoash that began with such excitement ends ignobly. At the age of forty-seven, after forty years on the throne, he is "buried with his fathers," and the house of YHWH that nurtured him and the welfare of which he, in turn, championed stands emptied of its treasure.

Chapter 17

YHWH DELIVERS JEHOAHAZ OF ISRAEL
FROM ARAM

2 Kings 13:1-9

Backing up to the twenty-third year of Jehoash, the narrator introduces Jehoahaz son of Jehu of Israel. It was in the same twenty-third
year that Jehoash instituted his new system for temple repairs (12:7).
Is there any link? Did Jehu's death that year have repercussions in
Judah, liberating Jehoash to reform his priesthood's responsibilities?
Whatever the historical reality, the literary concurrence of the two
events seems key to the narrator whose own synchronisms with Jehoash of Judah contradict this dating. On the one hand, v. 1 attributes
to Jehoahaz a seventeen-year reign, yet on the other, v. 10 begins the
reign of his son in the thirty-seventh year of Jehoash of Judah, leaving
him with a fourteen year reign. From a historical point of view, one solution would be to posit a three-year co-regency with his father Jehu.[9]
But the text itself offers no such clue, foregrounding instead the repetition of the twenty-third year as a time of change in both South and
North.

The evaluation of Jehoahaz's reign is thoroughly negative. In v. 2
the formulaic divine perspective ("he did what was bad in the eyes of
the LORD") is followed by the equally standard formulation that he followed in the sinful footsteps of Jeroboam, Israel's arch-sinner. His own
father, Jehu, who had rid Israel both of the hated house of Ahab and
Baal worship, is not the standard of comparison but the original northern dynast, Jeroboam.

---

[9] This is one suggestion of Cogan and Tadmor, *II Kings*, 142.

The events of Jehoahaz's reign are summarized in highly theological fashion without any of the earthy and earthly details that give other accounts their verisimilitude. In fact, the text appears modeled after the formulaic summaries of the book of Judges (see, for example, Judg 2:7-11). YHWH's anger causes him to give Israel "into the hand" of its enemy, but Jehoahaz pleaded with YHWH who listened, saw, and sent a savior (*môšiʿa*). They "went out of the hand" of the enemy and "dwelled in their tents." In this case the named enemy is Aram led by Hazael and his son Ben-hadad. The perennial raider Hazael here becomes YHWH's agent for punishing his people who, in the formula, have replaced the king as the object of YHWH's wrath. And Jehoahaz, for all of his sinfulness, recognizes the divine causation of the Aramean attacks, for he beseeches YHWH. No battles are described, no specific cities are taken, no tribute is offered to Hazael. With its archaizing terminology such as "savior" and "tents," this account transforms the Aramean war into a replay of an ancient battle, an exemplum of YHWH's anger, punishment, and mercy. At the end we hear of the pathetic force left to Jehoahaz, as if the divinely inspired Aramean plague had passed and he was counting his losses.

That is all there is of Jehoahaz. He is a name attached to a snippet of a morality story. If there were more in the Chronicles of the Kings of Israel, which our author cites, he chose not to include it. After his father Jehu, in whose tumultuous tale the writer revels, Jehoahaz seems to have made no impression of his own and is cast into a lifeless narration.

Chapter 18

DYING ELISHA PROMISES JOASH OF ISRAEL
VICTORY OVER ARAM

2 Kings 13:10-25

The regnal summary of Joash of Israel is a bland reflection of that of his lackluster father. Like him he followed in the tradition of Jeroboam (v. 11) and so displeased YHWH. Tantalizing, though, is the reference to his "heroism *(gĕbûrātô)*" in a battle with Amaziah of Judah whose story has not yet been told. Is this a gap to be filled in or a blank without any follow-up? For the moment we cannot know, for the narrator turns immediately to Joash's death and burial (v. 13).

Yet this is not the last we hear of Joash. Although his reign has been formally closed, he takes on flesh only afterwards, in the final tale of Elisha and in the story of Amaziah of Judah. At first glance, it seems inconsistent to close Joash's reign and then immediately reintroduce him in an encounter with Elisha. Yet the countervailing demands of the Elisha tale determine this arrangement. Just as Elisha's assumption of the prophetic role (2 Kings 2) took place outside any royal file, so too does his death. This placement suggests that Elisha is not under the thumb of any king, that his power operates independently of royal authority. So in Elisha's final appearance, Joash becomes a creature of his tale rather than the reverse.

Subject-verb order ("Elisha had taken ill") reverses narrated time, turning back into Joash's reign, and reintroduces Elisha, who has been absent from the narrative since sending his disciple to Jehu (9:1). Not his location but his sickness unto death is the subject of the first verse (v. 14) and the reason Joash goes to see him. The king who has been given no voice during the summary of his reign steps out of the shadow to acclaim the dying prophet. Despite the formulaic sinfulness attributed to Joash, his behavior here bespeaks a different man. Weeping and crying forth, "My father, my father! The chariots of Israel and its horsemen!" he greets Elisha. This acclamation, we recall, was earlier addressed to Elijah by Elisha himself as Elijah ascended in the chariot and horses of fire (2:12). Why the repetition of this cry? When Elisha uttered it, he described the situation that he witnessed; Elijah was his prophetic "father," and a fiery chariot was taking him away. But Elisha too is associated with the surreal phenomenon of horses and chariots of fire (6:17). Or, in Joash's mouth, does the phrase denote Elisha's protection of Israel, now in jeopardy because of his mortal illness? In terms of overall structure, the repetition of the cry associates Elisha once again with Elijah, affirming at the end of Elisha's career his discipleship to Elijah.

Elisha reacts as if Joash were asking for prediction and protection and offers two symbolic actions that issue in oracles. Though the illness of Elisha is not described, he would seem to be bedridden, asking Joash to do those things that he cannot do himself. Elisha issues a set of imperatives to Joash, whose unquestioning obedience is conveyed by the narrator's repetition of the same verbs that Elisha uses. The first action, shooting an arrow out the window to the east, after having had his hands touched by Elisha, is interpreted by Elisha as a pre-enactment of victory over Aram. As in the resuscitation of the dead boy, Elisha's body parts, when touched to the subject's, transfer to the subject Elisha's energy. The second action is more ambiguous. Told to strike the ground with the arrows, Joash obeys, but then Elisha becomes angry when Joash stops after three strikes. As a result, Elisha qualifies the total victory promised when the arrow was shot. Now Joash will not defeat Aram totally (*ʿad-kallēh*, vv. 17, 19), but only three times, as symbolized by the three arrows. Joash's innocent infraction thus justifies the ongoing warfare with Aram despite Elisha's prediction of total victory.

The death of Elisha is reported without fanfare (v. 20a). For him there is no supernatural translation as there was for Elijah. Yet a posthumous incident, unique in the Tanakh, expresses the belief that death did not totally defeat him. With a verb in the imperfect ("they would come"), the writer tells of the habitual raids of the Moabites and then shifts to a particular such raid that interrupted the burial of an Israelite man. Through the eyes of the Israelites we see the Moabites approach and feel the Israelites' complete surprise as they toss the corpse into Elisha's grave. If the burial party was surprised at the appearance of the Moabites, the reader is surprised at the resurrection of the dead man when he touches Elisha's bones. Neither witnesses (who, in any case, seem to have made a quick departure) nor narrator comment on this miracle. But just as Gehazi reminds the king of Elisha's resuscitation of the Shunammite woman's son, this final Elisha episode confirms that revivifying power again. Like relics, his bones in death perform what his body accomplished in life. Elisha exits but his power lives on. If Elijah's death is unique, so too is Elisha's "afterlife."

Elisha's prophecy that Israel would defeat Aram three times occasions the placement of the next section (vv. 22-25). This narration reviews Israel's recent subjugation to Aram and culminates in the fulfillment of the prophecy. A summary statement first declares that Hazael oppressed Israel during the entire reign of Jehoahaz. But this seems to trigger a conflict with the earlier claim that Jehoahaz's pleas to YHWH caused him to lift the Aramean stranglehold by means of a *môšî͑a* (vv. 4-5). Was it during the reign of Jehoahaz or his son Joash that the defeat of the Arameans occurred? In the earlier passage, the timing of YHWH's deliverance is not specified, and oppression continues under Hazael's son Ben-hadad (v. 3). So if our passage is reread in light of the earlier one, recovery of the cities lost to Hazael and Ben-hadad by Joash, son of Jehoahaz (vv. 24-25), would be the deliverance earned by Jehoahaz's pleas. Thus YHWH's response is delayed by one generation. So far we have two causes for the Aramean defeat: YHWH's response to Jehoahaz's intercession and Joash's obedience to Elisha's symbolic enactment.

But a third cause emerges from our passage. Most unusually, the covenant with Abraham, Isaac, and Jacob is invoked as the reason for YHWH's being "gracious and merciful" (v. 23).[10] "And he would not consent to their destruction, and he has not cast them from before his face until now." This chronological bridge extends the theological significance of YHWH's salvation until the writer's day. Though one would presume that the writer lived after the destruction of the North, the "until now" suggests that he wants to stress the salvific persistence of YHWH.

Three parallel lines of causation, all conveying divine control, thus meet in the victory over Aram. Yet immediately after resorting to the most directly theological of them (v. 23), the narrator shifts to a fourth and utterly prosaic cause. Son takes from son what father had taken from father. The fact of the three defeats is then reported without confirmation that it represents the fulfillment of prophecy. The narration moves from omniscient insight into YHWH's motives to pure journalistic reportage.

From a broader literary perspective, we should note that just as the second part of 2 Kings (8:7–13:25) began with Elisha entering the political

---

[10] The patriarchs are mentioned together in 1–2 Kings only here and in 1 Kgs 18:36, where the phrase is "Abraham, Isaac, and Israel."

realm and fomenting revolution in Aram and Israel, revolution that spills over into Judah as well, so too it ends with Elisha promising victory over Aram and with that victory affirmed by the narrator. So although the organization of the narrative according to the reigns of the kings persists, the prophetic dimension has determined the larger structure of the narrative in both Parts One and Two.

EXCURSUS

The Relationship of the Elisha Tales to the Elijah Tales

Having followed the sequence of the Elisha stories as the substance of Part One and observed the framing function of Elisha's appearances in Part Two, I want to pause to consider the Elisha cycle of stories as a whole, particularly in relationship to the Elijah cycle that precedes it in 1 Kings. As a collection of prophet stories the Elisha cycle is unique in Kings and, for that matter, in the Tanakh as a whole both because of the number of episodes in general and of miracle tales in particular. Unique as well is the linking of Elisha to Elijah: no other two prophets are so connected. None of the other named prophets, as represented in the books of both the Early and Later Prophets, have contact with each other. They are lone operators whose powers are non-transferable. Yet the text of 1–2 Kings, in both direct and subtle ways, aims to portray Elisha as the successor to Elijah.

Most emphatically, two episodes unambiguously establish the succession. After the eerie tale of Elijah's encounter with YHWH at Horeb, YHWH orders Elijah to find and anoint Elisha to be a prophet after him (1 Kgs 19:16-17), and Elijah, in the next scene, casts his mantle upon him (19:19-21). Elisha then drops from sight until he is depicted accompanying Elijah on his final journey, despite the latter's repeated admonitions, and requesting a double portion of his spirit before Elijah ascends (2 Kgs 2:1-18). Elisha's subsequent miracles, as we have seen, confirm that he received what he asked for and is thus regarded as the legitimate prophetic heir of Elijah.

A second way in which Elisha is linked to Elijah is by Elisha's fulfillment of the final commission given to Elijah, the order to anoint Hazael as king of Aram and Jehu as king of Israel (1 Kgs 19:15-16). Elisha, not Elijah, is credited with instigating the coups that brought these two upstarts to power. Yet the narrative evinces no recognition of the discrepancy between the prophet commanded and the prophet who fulfills the commission. (Only in connection with Jezebel's murder is Elijah cited by name as the source of the prophecy that predicted her demise [2 Kgs 9:36-37]). Elijah is never directly faulted for failing to accomplish his mission nor is Elisha criticized for taking matters into his own hands. The effect of the linkage is to create prophetic continuity that keeps YHWH's word alive over two careers.

Third, the succession of Elisha is established by specific affirmations. Immediately after Elijah's ascent, for instance, when Elisha tests his powers by casting Elijah's mantle to part the Jordan river, the prophetic disciples confess, "The spirit of Elijah rests upon Elisha" (2 Kgs 2:14). The private confession is followed shortly by a public acclamation when a servant of the king of Israel identifies Elisha as "one who poured water on Elijah's hands" (3:11). This recollection of Elisha's service authenticates him as a prophet of YHWH.

A link between the two sets of stories can also be traced in their frequently common subject matter. Both prophets feed widows (1 Kgs 17:8-16; 2 Kgs 4:1-7), resuscitate dead boys (1 Kgs 17:17-24; 2 Kgs 4:8-37), and send oracles to mortally ill kings (2 Kgs 1; 8:7-15). These duplicated motifs may be the literary development of common type-scenes or of recasting tales associated with one prophet for the other. It is odd, for instance, that the destitute widow of 1 Kgs 17:8-16, whose son Elijah revives, has a house big enough to contain an upstairs room. Yet the integral function of an upstairs room in the house of the wealthy Shunammite, whose son Elisha brings back to life, suggests that the Elijah episode developed out of the Elisha tale.

Even more interesting is the pattern of story sequences between the two cycles. Nearly every Elijah episode is echoed in some way in a corresponding Elisha episode—and in the same order. These parallels may be diagramed as follows:

Elijah cycle—1 Kings	Elisha cycle—2 Kings
17:2-6 Elijah drinks from a wadi	3:9-20 Israel drinks from a wadi
17:8-16 Elijah multiplies oil and grain for widow	4:1-7 Elisha multiplies oil for a widow
17:17-24 Elijah resuscitates boy	4:8-37 Elisha resuscitates boy
18:20-39 Famine and the true God; miracle precipitates conversion	5:1-27 Leprosy and the true God; miracle precipitates conversion
19:1-3 Pursuit of Elijah; oath by pursuer	6:8-14, 31-32 Pursuit of Elisha; oath by pursuer
21:1-29 False witness denies man his land by royal directive	8:1-6 True witness rewards woman her land by royal directive
2 Kgs 1:1-18 Elijah sends oracle to mortally ill king	8:7-15 Elisha sends oracle to mortally ill king

The first correspondence involves stories of drought and famine in which water is provided in a wadi by divine intervention, for Elijah in the first tale and for the troops and animals of Israel and Judah in the second. Next are two stories of the prophet's miraculous provision of resources for a poverty-stricken widow, each followed by a tale of miraculous revival of a dead boy, in the case of Elijah the son of the same widow just provided for. Both Elisha episodes celebrate the thaumaturgy of the man of God, while the corresponding Elijah tales stress the power of YHWH behind the miracle.

The drama on Mount Carmel, the great contest between Elijah and the prophets of Baal to determine the identity of the true God, has no exact analogue among the Elisha tales, yet the story of Naaman and Gehazi reiterates its theme in a lower key. Just as a king of Israel is powerless to deal with the famine devastating his people (1 Kgs 18:5), so too is another king of Israel unable to deal with the disease afflicting Naaman (2 Kgs 5:7). In both cases a prophet confronts royal impotence, sidelines the king, and takes charge of the situation himself. Elijah uses fire, Elisha water, but just as the former convinces his people that YHWH alone is God, the latter convinces Naaman of the same thing. And if the prophets of Baal are destroyed (1 Kgs 18:40), Gehazi, disloyal to his master, exits as a leper (2 Kgs 5:27). Both stories feature a miracle that results in the dramatic conversion of the afflicted: the people return to YHWH while Naaman turns to YHWH after the Jordan waters cure him.

Following these episodes come tales of pursuit. Jezebel hounds Elijah (1 Kgs 19:1-3), while the king of Aram (2 Kgs 6:8-14) and then the king of Israel (6:31-32) chase Elisha. Jezebel is enraged over the murder of her prophets, while the king of Aram is confounded by Elisha's clairvoyance that prevents his victory over Israel. Later, when Aram besieges Samaria, the king of Israel blames Elisha and takes an oath similar to the one Jezebel swears when she pursues Elijah (2 Kgs 6:31; 1 Kgs 19:2).

The next Elijah tale, the prophet's conflict with Ahab over his taking of Naboth's vineyard (1 Kgs 21) finds an interesting opposite in the episode in which a woman's land is restored to her. When Ahab cannot persuade Naboth to sell or trade his property adjoining the royal palace, Jezebel arranges to have false witnesses testify against Naboth, resulting in his execution and the royal appropriation of his land. The corresponding Elisha episode develops conversely. When the woman whose son Elisha had revivified returns from Philistine country and requests that her house and land be restored to her, Gehazi testifies to the king that she is the woman whose son Elisha had revivified, so the king restores her property to her. In the first case a woman, Jezebel, forces a man's disinheritance and his death; in the second, a man, Gehazi, supports a woman's inheritance and her life.

Elijah's final episode, before the scene of his departure, is a version of the mortally ill monarch type-scene which, as we have already seen earlier in the commentary, has a counterpart in the Elisha cycle. Here again the Elisha story reverses the Elijah tale, for whereas in the latter the king of Israel sends to a foreign god, Baal-zebub, for an oracle, in the former a foreign king, Ben-hadad, sends a messenger to the Israelite prophet for an oracle.

What this ordered set of correspondences suggests is a rather careful effort to portray Elisha and Elijah in tandem, to repeat and, in some cases, to augment Elijah's feats in the Elisha cycle. Elisha takes up the mantle of Elijah and the gauntlet and provides continued prophetic leadership. Without direction from either YHWH or Elijah, Elisha is shown instinctively seconding his master's acts. Does Elisha emerge as the better of the prophets because he has a double portion of prophetic spirit, works more wonders, and fulfills the political commission given by YHWH to Elijah (1 Kgs 19:15-16)? Or is Elijah, who acts only at YHWH's behest, calls upon YHWH for help, and is vouchsafed divine revelation and rapture, to be understood as the superior prophet? Or is the effect of the linkage to celebrate continuity and silence the conflict that may have existed historically between rival prophetic supporters? Or is ambiguity the aim or the effect?[11]

Unwilling to resolve those questions, let me offer instead a few historical observations that support the theological and esthetic nature of the linkage of the Elijah and Elisha cycles. First Elisha's career, as depicted, is improbably long. If he had succeeded Elijah early during the reign of Jehoram (2 Kgs 1:17–2 Kgs 2:1) and had continued through the reign of Joash (2 Kgs 13:13-14), he would have prophesied for more than fifty years. Second, Elisha's connection to all of the kings but Joash seems quite tenuous. In those few stories in which he deals directly with the "king of Israel," the king's name is not mentioned at all (e.g., 2 Kgs 5:5-8; 6:26; 8:3-6) or only peripherally (2 Kgs 3:6). Elisha's tie to Jehoram, the monarch on the throne when he succeeds Elijah, appears especially problematic. While Elisha is shown, on the one hand, supporting Jehoram in his battles against Moab (2 Kings 3) and Aram (2 Kgs 6:8-23), he is portrayed, on the other hand, instigating Jehoram's downfall at the hand of Jehu (2 Kgs 9:1-3).[12] If Elisha supported Jeho-

[11] The advertisement for a new book, which I have not yet seen, promises a different answer to these questions. Wesley J. Bergen, *Elisha and the End of Prophetism.* JSOT Supplement Series 286 (Sheffield: Sheffield Academic Press, 1999).

[12] For a discussion of the dating issues see Alexander Rofé, *The Prophetical Stories* (Jerusalem: The Magnes Press, 1988) 7–74.

ram, why would he conspire to overthrow him? Furthermore, the tales of Elisha ignore the battle against the worship of Baal waged by Elijah during the reigns of the Omride kings. And the depiction of Elisha's instigation of the Jehuite anti-Baal revolution in Israel minimizes his role, focusing instead on that of the anonymous prophetic disciple. This agent is shown acting independently of Elisha by fashioning his own oracle (2 Kgs 9:6-10) based on the prophecy not of Elisha, but Elijah.

These observations raise the suspicion that the Elisha stories were originally not connected to the Omride kings at all but were set later, during the reign of the Jehuite kings, by which time the Baalists had been defeated.[13] Only the effort to link Elijah with Elisha, to connect two legendary wonder workers, then, would have caused the resetting of the latter's stories in a time period in which they do not well fit. The various kinds of literary connections and parallels we have noted thus came to cement in literary form a claim of succession that likely had no historical warrant. By thus creating a dynamic pair of prophets that span the Omride dynasty, the writer could show the ongoing power of YHWH both to fight against the supporters of Baal and to support the fight against poverty and injustice.

[13] This is the conclusion of Rofé, 74.

Part Three

TURMOIL AND TRAGEDY
FOR ISRAEL
2 Kings 14–17

Chapter 19

AMAZIAH OF JUDAH AND JOASH OF ISRAEL

2 Kings 14:1-22

Although he now turns to the reign of Amaziah of Judah, the contemporary of Joash of Israel, the writer keeps the focus on the North by staging Joash's interaction with the southern king. The warfare between the two alluded to in 13:12, is to be explained now in its proper place in the account of Amaziah's reign. But that comes a bit later. Before any particulars are given, the reign as a whole is evaluated—ambivalently it would appear. On the one hand, "he did what was right in the LORD's eyes" (v. 3). On the other hand, his acts were comparable not to David's but to those of his father Jehoash. Indeed, just like Jehoash he did not interfere with the offerings at the *bamôt* (v. 4).

With these preliminary, standard generalities out of the way, the unique events of Amaziah's reign come to light. First among them is vengeance against the assassins of his father. The priority of this action is expressed in the *wayĕhî* ("and so it was") clause of v. 5a: "As soon as the kingdom was secure in his hand." He wasted no time in taking vengeance once he had the power to do so. Yet by leading with the direct object in v. 6 ("But the sons of the assassins he did not slay"), the narrator stresses Amaziah's refusal to take vengeance against the next generation. This departure from the standard practice of blood vengeance is justified in terms of Deuteronomic law, quoted directly from Deut 24:16 (v. 6). Why is this law, which insists that parents and children not be put to death for each other's sins, quoted here? Besides its applicability to the case at hand, it may be intended to sound a broader theme. Amaziah is assassinated like his father, we hear later, but because of his own deeds, not his father's. Then too, the ultimate defeat of Israel, this law implies, should not be attributed to the fathers' sins.

Amaziah's restraint comes as an exemplum of divine restraint in YHWH's dealings with his people.

Next a major military victory over Edom is epitomized in a single verse (v. 7). Historically this battle may have been part of a campaign to reclaim the Arabah (the rift valley between the Dead Sea and the Gulf of Aqaba) and the approaches to the Red Sea in the wake of the political shakeups following the Assyrian defeat of Aram-Damascus. But the text gives no hint of the political or economic significance of the battle, remarking instead on the change of name of the captured city of Sela to Joktheel and the persistence of the name until the writer's time. This lack of concern with the larger international situation is typical of Kings which includes mention of such events only insofar as they contribute to an evaluation of the king in question.

In this case, for instance, the mention of the victory over Edom functions to explain Amaziah's arrogant challenge of the superior forces of Israel. With the conjunction ʾaz ("then"), the narrator links Amaziah's victory both temporally and consequentially to his provocative message to Joash (v. 8): "Then Amaziah sent messengers to Jehoash son of Jehoahaz son of Jehu, king of Israel saying, 'Let us confront each other (*nitrāʾeh pānîm*).'" Joash's identification is longer than the message. The inclusion of his lineage back to the divinely favored Jehu conveys a rock-solid monarchy and hints at the folly of Amaziah's challenge. The phrase *nitrāʾeh pānîm,* found only here and in the corresponding verse in 2 Chr 25:17, does not necessarily connote hostile intentions, but Joash correctly interprets it so.

Previously, we saw Joash's loyalty to Elisha; now we see his wisdom. Trying to avoid battle with Amaziah, he responds to him with a wisdom parable in which a thistle requests from a cedar the cedar's daughter as a wife for the thistle's son. The cedar does not respond; instead a wild beast tramples down the thistle. Clearly Amaziah is being compared to the thistle who overreaches himself in his request and is destroyed as a result. The identification is clinched by the repetition within the parable of the verb *šalaḥ* ("he sent") predicated of Amaziah in v. 8. The thistle expresses the arrogance with which Joash charges Amaziah in Joash's own interpretation of the parable.

In his explanation of the parable Joash is revealed as a shrewd analyst: "You have certainly defeated Edom," he begins, acknowledging the facts of the case and his own recognition of Amaziah's accomplishments (v. 10). But having offered praise, he then criticizes what he sees to be the consequence of that victory: "you have lifted up your heart." Then he offers advice: "Be honored, stay home. Why flirt with evil and fall—you and Judah along with you?" On the one hand, he recognizes Amaziah's accomplishments and sees him as deserving of honor. On the other hand, he threatens defeat if Amaziah interferes with him. As in the parable, in which not the cedar addressed by the thistle, but rather some "beast of the field" is the cause of the trampling of the thistle, so too here Joash does not identify himself as the one who will bring Amaziah down. The threat is veiled. The "falling" is almost portrayed as a natural consequence of the "lifting" of his heart.

Only Joash speaks here; Amaziah does not respond. Instead the narrator summarizes: "he did not hear." Now the phrase "and they saw each others' faces," repeated in v. 11, clearly denotes hostile confrontation. Joash's preemptive strike (*wayya'al*) results in the defeat and fleeing of "Judah" before "Israel." The specifics of the battle are skipped in favor of the bare mention of the global victory of North over South. By contrast, Joash's punitive actions against the king, the capital, and the royal treasury are each described. The importance of Joash's capture of King Amaziah is underscored by the identification of Amaziah in terms of his lineage and by the inversion of verb and direct object: "Amaziah . . . Joash captured" (v. 13). Yet we are not told of Amaziah's fate at Joash's hands. One also wonders what gold, silver, and other treasures Joash could have plundered since Amaziah's father had shipped everything off as tribute to Hazael of Aram not many years before (12:18-19). In all of this retribution, including the taking of hostages, Joash is not criticized. Indeed, wisdom is issued in his voice, while Amaziah is shown paying the price of his folly. The account concludes with the confirmation that Joash "returned to Samaria," without conquering Judah. Unlike Amaziah who was not satisfied with his victory over Edom, Joash defeats Amaziah and departs.

In vv. 15-16 the reign of Joash is summarized again, repeating 13:12-13. This odd repetition in the middle of Amaziah's reign testifies to the importance of Joash in the account of Amaziah. Since it is Joash whose voice is dominant, it is his reign, now having been explicated in further detail, that must be tied off first before proceeding to conclude Amaziah's. Still, it is curious that Joash gets buried twice with 14:15-16 repeating nearly verbatim 13:12-13. The only noteworthy addition is the naming of his successor, Jeroboam, now that Joash exits from the narrative for good. The replay of Joash's death does serve as a springboard for the unusual formulation that Amaziah survived him by fifteen years, which in turn leads to the report of Amaziah's own death.

Like his father, Amaziah is portrayed as the victim of a conspiracy by unnamed assassins. His fleeing (*wayyānās*) before them echoes the recent fleeing (*wayyānusû*) of Judah before Israel (v. 12). Earlier Amaziah had "lifted up (*ûněśā'akā*) his heart" and brought defeat upon himself. Now they "lift up (*wayyiśě'û*)" his corpse on horses to transport the murdered king back to the family tomb in Jerusalem (v. 20).

These word echoes contribute to a sense of completion in an otherwise unremarkable literary epitaph. His successor, on the other hand, is introduced in an unusual way, not by "his son so-and-so reigned after him," but by an enthronement by "all the people of Judah." This statement of the popular acclamation of the sixteen-year-old Azariah seems meant to counter well-founded suspicions of conflict among rival claimants to the throne following Amaziah's assassination. Indeed the narrator cannot wait until the account of Azariah's reign officially begins to begin singing his praises, crediting him here with the rebuilding of the Red Sea port of Elath.

Chapter 20

JEROBOAM RESTORES ISRAEL'S TERRITORY

2 Kings 14:23-29

The second King Jeroboam of Israel, whose deeds and infamy resound through the denunciations of the prophet Amos, receives scant attention despite his long forty-one year reign. After the formulaic comparison of his sinfulness to that of his namesake, Jeroboam ben Nebat, the second Jeroboam's great territorial conquests are summarily enumerated. With parallel inverted word order phrasing, the narrator implicitly compares his accomplishments with those of his contemporary, Azariah. Just as "he [Azariah] rebuilt (*hû' bānāh*, v. 22)," so too "he [Jeroboam] restored (*hû' hēšîb*, v. 25)." No mean feat this, the restoration of the borders of Israel from Lebo-hamath in the north to the Dead Sea in the south. But though the verse begins by touting Jeroboam's achievement, it ends by crediting divine causation.

The writer announces that Jeroboam's expansion of Israelite territory constitutes the fulfillment of a prophetic word to the prophet Jonah ben Amittai, but neither prophet nor word has entered the narrative previously. So this information comes as a surprise, a gap in our knowledge closing just as it is being opened, a prophet named only at the moment that his prophecy is enacted. Trying, futilely, to recall when this prophecy was uttered, one remembers instead the series of direct divine interventions that have powered the dynasty of Jehu. First, Elisha's prophetic word brought Jehu to power (9:1-3), while YHWH, speaking directly to Jehu, promised him a five-generation dynasty (10:31). To his son Jehoahaz YHWH sent a "savior *(môšiaᶜ),*" for YHWH "saw *(rā'āh)*" Israel's suffering (13:4-5). Then to grandson Joash Elisha delivers another oracle promising limited victory over Aram (13:15-19), and the narrator confirms YHWH's grace and mercy based on the covenant with the patriarchs. Now to the fourth generation, Jeroboam, another prophet speaks and YHWH again "saw" (*rāʾāh*, 14:26) Israel's bitterness and "delivered *(wayyôšîʿēm)*" Israel through Jeroboam (v. 27). Indeed, the identification of Jeroboam as deliverer suggests that he is the one promised to Jehoahaz who would defeat Aram once and for all. And Jeroboam does exactly that by recovering Damascus and Hamath (v. 28). In the evaluations of all four generations divine intentionality is represented explicitly through the narrator's or YHWH's voice. In particular the Hebrew verb *hôšîaʿ* ("deliver") expresses YHWH's direct management of Israelite fate in the accounts of the successors of Jehu (13:5, 17; 14:27). Although the narrative ultimately leads to the defeat of Israel, there is a repeated emphasis on the special favor shown to Jehu's dynasty and on YHWH's unwillingness to countenance Israel's destruction. Furthermore, the surprise recurrence to a hitherto unreferenced prophet highlights the importance of the prophecy-fulfillment structure that transcends the dominant regnal structure in 2 Kings. Even as the narrative leapfrogs back and forth in time and northward and southward in space and even out to Aram and Edom, the word of YHWH moves steadily forward plotting the fates of both Israelite kingdoms.

Chapter 21

COUPS IN ISRAEL BUT STABILITY IN JUDAH

2 Kings 15:1-38

Despite the excesses of Jehu, the writer has been at pains to demonstrate and proclaim the favor shown by YHWH to his heirs on the throne. Even in the account of Judah's king Amaziah, Jehu's grandson, Joash, steals the stage, reappearing in the story of his contemporary after his own reign is already closed off (13:13). Jeroboam's long and prophetically confirmed career caps the divinely graced existence of Israel during the reign of Jehu's dynasty. With Jeroboam's death, however, begins the portrayal of an Israel racked with coups and counter-coups preceding its ultimate destruction. The rapidity and darkness of that plunge is conveyed through a series of short regnal summaries in which no dramatization halts the narrator's voice. These are framed by accounts of long-reigning kings of Judah whose steadiness highlights the turmoil in the North.

Azariah of Judah (15:1-7)

In contrast to the full and fascinating account by the Chronicler (2 Chr 26:1-23) of both the achievements and the arrogance of this king (whom the Chronicler calls Uzziah), our text tells nearly nothing. What stands out as a result is the extraordinary length of Azariah's reign— fifty-two years—during part of which time his son Jotham served as co-regent, because of Azariah's leprosy. That is, this truncated report conveys the Judahite stability against which Israelite calamity will be drawn.

Azariah is introduced as a carbon copy of his father with the stereo-typed description of 15:1-4 replicating nearly precisely the pattern of 14:1-4. The sole difference is that unlike Amaziah, Azariah is not com-pared negatively to David. The sole significant action of Azariah's reign is attributed to YHWH. His contraction of leprosy is understood as a divine plague, an affliction delivered by YHWH himself. Whereas the Chronicler explains this disease as divine punishment for Uzziah's brazen offering of incense to YHWH in the face of priestly prerogative (2 Chr 26:16-20), 2 Kings skips over Azariah's dastardly defiance and simply announces the result: "And he was leprous until the day of his death" (15:5). Without an acknowledged motivation, YHWH's plague seems arbitrary or somehow connected to Azariah's toleration of the *bamôt*. Yet other similarly tolerant kings were not so plagued. The ef-fect of this blank is to focus attention on the consequence: the exit of Azariah to separate quarters and the entrance of his son Jotham into the role of ruler over the "people of the land." Despite the incapacity of the king to govern, continuity is assured by Jotham "governing *(šopēṭ)*." With Jotham in place, the text quickly proceeds to the formulaic end of Azariah's reign, leaving unanswered questions about the timing of Jotham's assumption of responsibilities and his relationship to his ail-ing father.

Zechariah of Israel (15:8-12)

The final monarch in the dynasty of Jehu gets short shrift. As king for only six months, he does not merit description beyond the formu-laic. Only his demise is of interest, for he is the victim of a conspiracy, just recompense for a dynasty that assumed power in the same way. That judgment is expressed in the narrator's retrospective following the standard close of the regnal description. Recalling YHWH's promise to Jehu that there would be four generations of his descendants on the throne, the narrator both justifies the short reign of Zechariah and draws the curtain on this exceptional period of divine favor.

Shallum of Israel (15:13-15)

Both the reign of Shallum and its accounting in the text are even briefer than those of Zechariah. As if he were afraid of losing track of this one-month monarch altogether, the narrator reverses the formula of accession, "In the *nth* year of *y, z* became king," in order to lead off with Shallum's name: "Shallum ben Yavesh became king in the thirty-ninth year of King Uzziah of Judah" (v. 13). And his name is about all we know of him. There is not even time to castigate him for following in the sins of Jeroboam! No sooner is he installed in office and in the text than his assassin appears and takes him out. One Menahem ben Gadi from Tirzah "goes up" to Samaria, kills Shallum, and takes his place as king all in one verse. As for Shallum his concluding summary remembers him only as a conspirator against Zechariah, YHWH's agent for ending Jehu's dynasty.

Menahem of Israel (15:16-22)

Before the story of Menahem's reign officially begins, a verse set off in the Hebrew as a separate paragraph relates his defeat of a town called Tiphsah (usually read Tappuah), his massacre of its inhabitants, and the ripping open of its pregnant women. The loose coordination with his overthrow of Shallum ("Then *[ʾāz]* Menahem smote Tiphsah") suggests parallel timing, perhaps that he attacked the town on the way from Tirzah to Samaria in a march of terror. By the same token, the placement of this note before Menahem's royal file opens indicates its occurrence before his kingship begins. Though related without explicit editorial judgment this preview of the next king expresses horror at his behavior through the use of the evocative verb *biqqēʿa* ("ripped open," v. 16).

The formal account of Menahem's reign gives further expression to his moral failings. To the standard formula attributing to him the sins of Jeroboam is appended the amplifier "all his days" (v. 18). And the portrayal of his reaction to the invasion of Assyria is that of a self-serving despot. The significance of that invasion, the first by the power that will soon destroy Israel, is heralded by the unusual and abrupt opening with the Hebrew verb in the perfect: "Came Pul, king of Assyria, against the land" (v. 19). Pul, a nickname in late sources for Tiglath-Pileser III, receives no introduction; his was clearly a household name for the writer and his original audience. Menahem, rather than opposing the invader, enlists his support by forking over the enormous sum of one thousand talents of silver. In return, Pul is "to be his hands with him to strengthen the kingdom in his hand" (v. 19). Only after the "deal" is described do we hear that the source of the silver was not the royal treasury but rather the *gibbôrê ḥayil* ("men of substance"), probably the landed gentry. By specifying the amount levied from each man—fifty shekels of silver—the writer clearly emphasizes Menahem's rapacity. Menahem's scheme apparently works; Tiglath Pileser leaves Israel without destroying it and Menahem's "hands" are strengthened sufficiently to permit a ten-year reign.

Pekahiah of Israel (15:23-26)

Menahem's dynastic pretensions are cut short only two years into the reign of his son Pekahiah when Pekahiah is assassinated by a group of conspirators headed by his deputy, Pekah. As in the summaries of the brief reigns of Zechariah and Shallum, the main point is not the reign but its overthrow. The quickened pace of coup and counter-coup racing toward Israel's end permits time for only a perfunctory bow to each king. What is included in this summary is the location of the assassination—the palace citadel, the participation of the Gileadites (from Gilead hailed Shallum and probably Menahem as well), and an ambiguous reference, perhaps to the hometowns of the conspirators (v. 25). Though we get the personal name of only the chief conspirator, because he succeeds Pekahiah as king, the inclusion of these place names bespeaks a desire to identify the source of the coup, to pin it down historically. Though dependent on formulaic summaries, the narrator is never entirely so. Each regnal account evinces some tilt of novelty, some feature that distinguishes it from all the rest. As they succeed each other in rapid succession, these particular details amid the stereotypical descriptions convey an air of historicity.

Pekah of Israel (15:27-31)

Pekah, a shortened form of the name Pekahiah, emerges as basically a carbon copy of his assassinated namesake. Though credited with a twenty-year rather than a two-year rule (but an alternative chronology also presents itself; cf. v. 30; 17:1), he, like Pekahiah, is the subject of no action, but rather the victim of a conspiracy. Yet the first Assyrian conquest and exile is assigned to his reign. Now in his official capacity as conqueror, Tiglath-Pileser is called by his official name and the cities and regions he took listed (v. 29). In a single word, without further explanation, the narrator names the policy that was to have such far-reaching implications for Israel: *wayyaglēm*, "he exiled them." Pekah, likely a Gileadite, who depended on Gileadites for his coup, now loses Gilead to Assyria, and his kingdom shrinks drastically in size. Sandwiched between the opening and closing parts of the bare-bones story of Pekah, this dramatic development is treated most undramatically. There is no reaction to it either by the king or the narrator, and no omniscient statement of divine causation brings it home as an object lesson.

Following the Assyrian entrance into Israel and into Pekah's regnal summary, the account concludes with a notice of the conspiracy that ends the reign. Here the coup leader's name is the only information given; neither location, confederation, nor motivation clutter the hurried report that Hoshea "conspired, . . . and struck, and killed" (v. 30).

Jotham of Judah (15:32-38)

At last we return to Judah after five kings of Israel come and go during the long reign of Azariah. Jotham, who, it was reported, "governed the people of the land" (v. 5) after his father was stricken with leprosy, now reigns on his own. Credited with a sixteen-year reign here (v. 33), he is assigned at least a twenty-year reign by the notice that Hoshea succeeded Pekah in Jotham's twentieth year (v. 31). To coordinate these two figures requires a four-year co-regency with his father Azariah. And a four-year co-regency would mean that Azariah was struck with leprosy quite late in life. Unfortunately 17:1 places Hoshea's succession in the twelfth year of Ahaz, Jotham's successor. However one tries to resolve these chronological inconsistencies, it is clear that dating itself is important to the writer's historical purpose.

The two pieces of information unique to Jotham both tie him to the temple. First, the name of his mother, Yerusha bat-Zadok, probably indicates priestly descent, suggesting that Jotham's regency during his father's lifetime had the support of the priestly establishment. Second, the only act attributed to Jotham is the building of the upper gate of the temple. Like his great-grandfather Jehoash, he is recognized for temple construction, perhaps because like him he is closely linked to the priests.

Just before the conclusion of Jotham's reign, just when the reader expects the comforting phrase about his death and burial, a report of divine intervention upsets the tranquillity. With the indefinite indicator "in those days *(bayyāmîm hāhēm)*" followed by a verb in the perfect tense ("began"), the narrator introduces the incursions into Judah by Rezin of Aram and Pekah of Israel (v. 37). Nearly the same phrase *(bîmê)* followed by another perfect verb, "came," introduced the invasion of

Tiglath-Pileser during the contemporaneous reign of Pekah (v. 29). The syntactic parallel suggests a relationship between the two invasions: Assyria's of Israel with Israel's and Aram's of Judah. Do Israel and Aram threaten Judah because of Assyria's advance? Are they looking for allies against Assyria? The book of Isaiah speaks to these questions (Isa 7:1-9), but no answers are forthcoming here. Instead divine causation is introduced. YHWH is named as the inciter of Rezin and Pekah, whereas divine causation was not invoked to explain the advance of Tiglath-Pileser.

The verb *hēḥēl* ("began") points ahead into the future in an ominous way. "In those days the LORD began to send forth against Judah . . ." (v. 37). As if to protect Jotham against the trouble that is coming, the narrator closes off his reign with a triple reference to "his fathers" in the otherwise formulaic conclusion: "Jotham slept with his fathers and he was buried with his father in the city of David his father."

Chapter 22

AHAZ OF JUDAH SUBMITS TO ASSYRIA

2 Kings 16:1-19

After the rapid summaries of eight reigns in succession, the narrative pace slows down to record with ominous detail the submission of King Ahaz of Judah to Assyria. Ahaz is pictured not only sending tribute to Tiglath-Pileser in exchange for his intervention against Aram and Israel, but also presiding over a cultic altar imported from Damascus. The material in this reign is arranged chiastically. Regnal summary at the beginning and the end surround descriptions of Ahaz's raiding of the temple treasures to pay off the Assyrian king. These descriptions, in turn, bracket instructions that Ahaz delivers to the priest Uriah for the construction of and worship at the new "great altar." At the center of the chiasm is a chilling image of apostasy as King Ahaz performs as priest before the new altar.

    A Regnal summary introduction (16:1-6)
       B King Ahaz sends tribute to King Tiglath-Pileser (16:7-9)
          C King Ahaz sends plans for altar from Damascus to
             priest Uriah who executes them (16:10-11)
            X King worships at the new great altar and moves the
               old bronze altar (16:12-14)
          C' King Ahaz commands the priest Uriah to offer sacrifices
             and he does so (16:15-16)
       B' King Ahaz raids the sancta of the temple because of the king
          of Assyria (16:17-18)
    A' Regnal summary conclusion (16:19-20)

A Regnal summary introduction (16:1-6)

Unlike that of nearly all of his Judahite predecessors, Ahaz's reign is evaluated negatively from the start. Instead of the typical positive opening statement that the king "did what was right in the eyes of the LORD," followed by negative qualifiers, Ahaz "did not do what was right in the eyes of the LORD." Only Joram, son of Jehoshaphat, merits the same woeful judgment—and for the same reason (8:18). Both are accused of following the customs of the kings of Israel, though Joram's marriage to the northern princess, Athaliah, is blamed for his waywardness. But Ahaz's sin is portrayed as even more weighty than this. Not only did he imitate Israelite kings, as if that would not be bad enough, but he sacrificed his own son as a burnt offering in the manner of the dispossessed nations of Canaan (v. 3). The criticism of Ahaz's cultic practices also goes well beyond the tolerance of the *bamôt*, the hilltop shrines, attributed to other kings of Judah. Ahaz is described actively worshiping there, in the stereotyped prophetic phrase, "on the hills and under every flourishing tree" (v. 4). The series of negative comparisons—his unlikeness to David and likeness to the kings of Israel and the dispossessed nations—makes Ahaz by far the most contemptible of the descendants of David ever to assume the throne. This image sets the stage for his willing subjugation to Assyria, presaging the worst fate yet for Judah.

Beginning with the phrase, "Then went up" (*ʾāz yaʿaleh*), the narrator shifts tenses in order to synchronize the entrance of the Aramean and Israelite enemies introduced during the reign of Jotham (15:37) with the reign of Ahaz (16:5). With their full titles, the kings' names separate the verb from its object as if to underscore the inevitability of this invasion. "Then went up—King Rezin of Aram and King Pekah son of Remaliah of Israel—on Jerusalem for war" (v. 5). Once the stage of Ahaz's evil has been set, it is time to bring in the enemies who have been waiting in the wings since the days of Jotham. The omniscient claim that "the LORD incited" is not repeated here, but the clear implication is that Ahaz's evil has brought them on.

The reason for the inability of the siege of Jerusalem to succeed is not given, but the vulnerability of Ahaz is underscored by the chronicling of the contemporaneous (*bāʿēt hahîʾ* ["at that time"], v. 6) capture of Elath by Rezin king of Aram (MT) or, more likely, Edom, and the driving out of Judahites and settlement by Edomites "until today." This chronological bridge makes the recapture of Elath into an aside, a "by the way," to explain how the current situation came to be.

B King Ahaz sends tribute to King Tiglath-Pileser (16:7-9)

The narrative present begins in v. 7 when, against the background sketched in v. 5, Ahaz appeals to Tiglath-Pileser for help. Quoted directly, Ahaz's message reveals something of his strategy. By identifying himself as "your servant and your son," Ahaz expresses both his subservience to and a professed formal filial dependence upon the Assyrian king. Hazael, appearing before Elisha, similarly refers to himself as "your servant" (8:13) and represents King Ben-hadad as "your son" (8:9). But by joining the two terms, a combination attested only here in the Bible, the writer conveys Ahaz's persuasive effort to draw the Assyrian king into Ahaz's war, to protect him as a father would a son.

Accompanying the messengers and the message goes a bribe (*šoḥad*). By using a term with clearly negative connotations (bribes are forbidden in the Torah [Exod 23:8; Deut 16:19] and attacked by prophets [e.g., Isa 5:23]), the writer criticizes Ahaz's raiding of temple and royal funds to pay for Tiglath-Pileser's intervention. Indeed information revealed earlier suggests that Tiglath-Pileser would have needed little urging to intervene. Menahem of Israel had already drawn him in to Israelite affairs by bribing him for support. And we know that the Assyrian king had captured cities and regions of the north during the reign of Pekah, Ahaz's northern contemporary. Having thus heard the result, we now learn the probable cause, picking up the action from the Judahite perspective. Tiglath-Pileser took those cities, we belatedly conclude, in response to Ahaz's request for help. In v. 9, however, it is the invasion not of Israel but of Aram that is narrated either because the conclusion just drawn is incorrect or because the writer does not want to tie Ahaz's bribe to the exile of Israelites. In either case, the result is that Damascus is defanged, Arameans exiled, and Rezin killed. In all of this Tiglath-Pileser is given no voice, no demands, no quid pro quo. The focus is on the initiative of Ahaz.

C King Ahaz sends plans for altar from Damascus to priest Uriah who executes them (16:10-11)

With Damascus in "friendly" Assyrian hands, Ahaz goes personally to greet his savior. In this section the characters are always called by their names and titles together—King Ahaz, Tiglath-Pileser king of Assyria, and Uriah the priest—underscoring the official nature of Ahaz's mission and its result. The initiative of Ahaz and silence of Tiglath-Pileser continues with all verbs in v. 10 predicated of Ahaz: "he went . . . he saw . . . he sent." For Ahaz seeing is believing: one look at the altar in Damascus apparently convinces him that he must have one too. Without recording Ahaz's reaction to the altar, the writer has him immediately send home to Uriah the priest both picture and plans. There is no indication that Tiglath-Pileser demanded that this altar be built to express Ahaz's vassalage; on the contrary, the swiftness of Ahaz's response suggests his personal enthusiasm, borne out in his upcoming ritual performance (vv. 12-13). Ahaz's eagerness to imitate and reproduce the Assyrian altar serves as another illustration of his following the ways of the nations. Verse 11 emphasizes through repetition the obedience and the speed with which the loyal priest Uriah executes the king's order and completes the altar even before Ahaz returns.

X King worships at the new great altar and moves the old bronze altar (16:12-14)

At the center of this enveloped narrative structure is the most dramatic picture: the king himself acting as priest offering sacrifices on the newly constructed altar. Almost in slow motion, the writer stages the scene: "The king came . . . the king saw . . . the king approached . . . and he ascended" (v. 12). Now he is not called King Ahaz but simply "the king," for it is his royal assumption of priestly prerogative that we watch as it unfolds. The silent ascent is followed by sacrificing, pouring, and throwing, a full complement of priestly activities here performed by the king (v. 13). Ahaz's piety before the new altar is followed by his relocation of the bronze altar. Here the writer fills in a gap opened only at the moment of its fulfillment: what had become of the original temple altar? Although the location of the bronze altar is not altogether clear in the Hebrew, the replacement of the old by the new certainly is. The writer expresses his critique of the king's "alteration" by spotlighting the demoted altar as the direct object syntactically: "And the bronze altar that was before YHWH he moved from before the house" (v. 14). The writer specifies that the bronze altar was "before the LORD," while the entire scene of the king's sacrifice does not specify YHWH as the addressee of his piety. The old Yahwistic altar has been displaced by a foreign model.

C' King Ahaz commands the priest Uriah to offer sacrifices and he does so (16:15-16)

As King Ahaz's second instruction to the priest Uriah, this section balances unit C where he delivered the order to build the altar. Here, as there, king and priest are identified both by name and title. The priest's obedience is underscored by the mirrored, framing clauses in v. 15 and v. 16: "And King Ahaz commanded Uriah the priest . . . . And Uriah the priest did everything that King Ahaz commanded." Within the frame is the longest speech in the narrative. Ahaz orders Uriah to perform habitually the rites that he has just performed inaugurally. Stringing together the various offerings as a series of direct objects of the verb "offer," the speech magnifies the importance of the rituals at what is now termed "the great altar." In contrast, Ahaz mentions the bronze altar almost as an afterthought at the very end of his speech and consigns it to his own private use, away from public display.

B' King Ahaz raids the sancta of the temple because of the king of Assyria (16:17-18)

Having replaced the bronze altar with an Assyrian model, Ahaz despoils the temple sancta for the purpose, as in unit B, of sending tribute to the king of Assyria. The report of this bribe in bronze, which would seem to have accompanied the bribe in gold and silver of v. 8, is triggered by the mention of the fate of the bronze altar. Again the writer conveys his critique of Ahaz's actions indirectly through the detailing of the despoliation and the remodeling of the access routes to the temple.

A' Regnal summary conclusion (16:19-20)

After the litany of reforms that Ahaz instituted following his return from Damascus, the story breaks off with an unremarkable formulaic regnal conclusion. Although the writer never directly chastises Ahaz for his actions in this conclusion, they well bear out the initial claim that "he did not do what was right in the eyes of the LORD" (v. 2).

Chapter 23

THE FALL OF ISRAEL AND ITS INTERPRETATION

2 Kings 17:1-23

The long chapter 17 comprises two narratives roughly equal in length and structure. The first briefly describes the defeat of Israel by the Assyrians and homiletically explains that defeat as divine punishment. The second tells the story of the foreigners brought to Israel by the Assyrians to replace the exiled Israelites and critiques the syncretistic religious practices in which these foreigners persisted. Interestingly, it is not the fate of the exiled Israelites but of the occupants of their repopulated land that concerns the writer. In both narratives the chief focus is the cultic perversion of the inhabitants of the North.

Hoshea of Israel provokes the Assyrian capture of Samaria (17:1-6)

The defeat of Israel is narrated without fanfare as the main item in the resumé of King Hoshea of Israel. No sooner is he introduced than the writer turns to the "facts" of Assyria's advance and eventual conquest of Samaria (vv. 3-6) followed by a theological justification (vv. 7-23). Hoshea's reign is never brought to official closure. The last we hear of him is his imprisonment by the king of Assyria (v. 4). This lack of closure underscores the absolute and final rupture caused by defeat and exile.

What little we are told about Hoshea does not prepare us for the catastrophe that is coming. As usual, the regnal summary begins with the date of the king's accession, though the length of his reign—nine years—is tagged on loosely, as if it hardly mattered. Ironically, this king is less condemned than any of his Northern predecessors: "He did bad in the eyes of the LORD but not like the kings of Israel who were before him." Though this judgment hints at some happy fate, the very next verse dashes those expectations. An altered word order underscores the irony: "Against *him* went up Shalmaneser king of Assyria" (v. 3). Despite Hoshea's better behavior toward YHWH, he is named as the target of the Assyrian king.

Faced with Shalmaneser's attack, Hoshea tries two strategies: initially tribute, eventually alliance with Egypt. The writer has us view Hoshea from the point of view of Shalmaneser who "found in Hoshea a conspiracy" (v. 4) when he discovered the Egyptian connection and failed to receive his annual tribute. Both Assyrian and Egyptian kings are called by name and title, while title-less Hoshea appears as an object tossed about between the two greater monarchs. By presenting Shalmaneser's perspective rather than his own, the writer avoids blaming Hoshea for the fate of the North; soon enough he will offer other justification. As for Hoshea's own fate, it is summarized in a sound play: *wayyaʿaṣrēhû* ("he arrested him") *wayyēʾasrēhû* ("he imprisoned him"). What became of him after his imprisonment is an unanswered question. While we might expect the narrative to run ahead to record Hoshea's fate, it stops short. Unlike Jehoiakin, the last scion of David taken into Babylonian exile, whose fate in Babylon is the subject of the last four verses of 2 Kings, Hoshea is never heard about again.

Verse 5 shifts from the personal to the national arena, from Hoshea to "all the land." This official account of the siege and capture of Samaria and the exiling of its inhabitants is essentially repeated in 18:9-11. Here the information is placed pointedly after the imprisonment of Hoshea suggesting that the imprisonment of the king preceded the three-year siege of Samaria. If Hoshea was imprisoned in his sixth year and he had been paying tribute "year by year" before that, it would appear that Hoshea's submission to Assyria must have begun early in his reign. If so, the Assyrian advance would have occurred during the contemporaneous reign of Ahaz who had requested Assyrian assistance against the Aramean-Israelite alliance. Thus, by inference, the report of the Assyrian dominance of Israel may be understood as completing the Assyrian response to Ahaz's request. Even though, historically, Shalmaneser took Samaria and his successor, Sargon II, handled the deportations of Israelites after Shalmaneser's death, this report does not name or distinguish these kings. Instead, the capture of the city and exile of its people are treated as swift and successive blows by a single unnamed king. What is important is not the process but the result: the resettlement of Israelites in several locations in Assyria, the names of which are meant to lend historicity to the account.

Theological explanation for catastrophe (17:7-23)

Opening with *wayĕhî* ("and thus"), v. 7 shifts into an interpretive mode, beginning a detailed explanation of Israelite sins that provoked Yнwн to cause Israel's defeat and exile. Whereas until this point Kings has focused on royal sins, here the blame for apostasy is placed squarely on the people as a whole: "And thus it happened because the people of Israel sinned against the Lord their God." Because calamity struck the nation as a whole, the writer imposes collective guilt upon it. Royal sins may have stirred Yнwн's wrath against particular kings and dynasties, but national catastrophe demands popular apostasy for an explanation.

The writer distances himself from the Northerners, always referring to them in the third person and to Yнwн as "their god." The "objective" perspective so created lends credence to the litany of sins next enumerated. With rhetorical flare the writer introduces those sins against the memory of the exodus from Egypt, the salvific act that ought to have inspired instead exclusive loyalty to Yнwн. The implication is that no sooner did Yнwн save them "from the land of Egypt, from under the hand of Pharaoh king of Egypt" (v. 7), than they began to sin. And not only did they worship other gods but followed the laws of those peoples whom Yнwн disinherited (vv. 8, 11), instead of, again by implication, the laws that Yнwн gave them. The guilt of the kings of Israel (v. 8) contributes to but is not solely responsible for the popular apostasy; the guilt falls upon the people as a whole. While in vv. 1-6 Hoshea's withholding of tribute is blamed for the Assyrian attack and eventual defeat of Israel, this section blames Israel's direct provocation of Yнwн. Without explaining Israel's motivation, the writer explicitly asserts that Israel acted precisely to anger Yнwн. They set up *bamôt*, pillars, and posts, offered sacrifices, and worshiped fetishes, flouting Yнwн's command, here quoted directly as, "Do not do this thing!" (v. 12).

Verse 13 divides Israel's history, in effect, into two sorry parts: the early period of rebellion and the later period of rebellion. Between them comes a directly quoted warning from Yнwн reported to have been delivered by "every prophet and every seer" to both Israel and Judah commanding return from their wicked ways. Against these are set explicitly "my commandments and my statutes, according to all the teaching that I commanded your fathers" (v. 13). Against the ways of the nations (*gôyim*) the voice of Yнwн sets his torah as taught by his prophets. Now Judah is included in the hearers, prolepetically suggesting that Judah will also be included in those condemned for not listening.

Next the narrator's voice (v. 14) responds to Yнwн's call for return by summarizing Israel's sins as a second rejection of God after the prophets' warnings. A second litany of misdeeds is prefaced by a comparison of the rebellious people with "their fathers" who also lacked faith in YHWH. Like their fathers they "stiffened their necks" (v. 14). The "objective" voice of the narrator gives way to an angry critique carried by a series of pungent verbs: they spurned, they were deluded, they forsook. Reference to the arch sin of the North, the building of the molten calves (by Jeroboam) and the worship of Baal, clearly directs this critique to Israel after the time of Jeroboam. Again the Israelites are accused of imitating the ways of the nations round about, but their cultic sins are detailed more specifically: augury, divination, child sacrifice (v. 17). Interestingly these practices have not been attributed before to the kings of the North, though they do derive from the Deuteronomist's picture of the abhorrent customs of the peoples of Canaan (Deut 18:9-10). The section concludes with the summary statement that "they sold themselves to do evil in the eyes of the LORD to anger him." Israel's behavior is thus viewed not as simple failure to obey but as active, spiteful provocation.

The concluding section (vv. 18-23) of the great indictment of Israel is unified by the thrice repeated refrain that YHWH banished Israel "from before his face" (vv. 18, 20, 23). The first statement of this refrain by itself (v. 18) seems a fitting ending to the homily just finished. Yet the mention that Judah, anachronistically termed "tribe," "alone remained" (v. 18) triggers a preview of the fate of the southern kingdom. Suddenly the narrative jumps ahead to the final fate of Judah which, like Israel, YHWH punishes in stages and finally casts out "from before his face" (v. 20). Judah is included with Israel as "all the seed of Israel" that YHWH rejects. Why does the writer leap forward in time, announcing the fate of Judah before he even relates its history as the sole remaining Israelite kingdom? Why does he permit this bad news to overshadow the upcoming positive stories of Kings Hezekiah and Josiah? The effect of this preview is to class Judah with Israel, to make it clear that although Israel met its end first, Judah's offenses against YHWH were no different from those of its northern neighbor. Divine control spanning centuries is underscored, while exilic and post-exilic Jewish readers can understand that despite the reformations of Hezekiah and Josiah, the die for Judah was cast before those good kings came on the scene.

Having linked Judah with Israel, the narrative now distinguishes them. Israel's disaster is blamed on its break with the house of David and the sins of Jeroboam. Israel and Jeroboam sinned mutually: they by making him king, he by leading them astray. The verb *sûr* ("turn away"), predicated of both Israel and YHWH, expresses a second mutuality: between Israel's not turning away from its sin and YHWH, in response, turning Israel away from before his face (vv. 22-23). Despite the momentary glance ahead at Judah's fate, the section ends with a ringing indictment of Israel alone for its following the sins of Jeroboam despite the prophets' warnings.

The very last statement of v. 23, the deportation of Israel to Assyria, repeats the information of v. 6. This repetition, an example of *Wiederaufnahme* ("repetitive resumption"), suggests that the theological explanation in vv. 7-23 functions midrashically, offering, as we have seen, an alternative explanation to that given in vv. 1-6 for the exile of Israel. In this extended midrash the agent of destruction is not the king of Assyria, but YHWH. The passive verb, "was exiled," states the circumstance following the report of YHWH's having "removed Israel from before his face" (v. 23). Finally, the narrator adds a chronological bridge "until today" making Israel's exile "from off its land" a current event and transforming history into admonition.

Foreigners in Israel and their syncretism (17:24-41)

Just as YHWH removed Israel "from before his face," so too the writer sends them into literary exile keeping his focus on the land that they vacated. Balancing the locations to which the Israelites were sent by the king of Assyria (v. 6) come the names of the cities from which the same unnamed king brings people to the land of Israel, here termed the "cities of Samaria" (v. 24), the Assyrian name for its new province. Quite clear is the fact that they are not merely temporary residents: "they took possession of Samaria and dwelled in its cities" (v. 24). They take the Israelites' place and inherit the land and its cities as the Israelites once did from the Canaanites. There is a finality about their settlement even if the stated agency is human (the king of Assyria), not divine.

Disclosing his own much later vantage point by the phrase "in the beginning of their dwelling there" (v. 25), the writer switches verb tense to describe the early religious situation when the inhabitants did not worship YHWH and when, in response, YHWH sent lions to kill them. Behind this little vignette is the assumption that YHWH comes with the territory, that anyone living in the land must fear him if they know what's good for them. Lions, we may note, are a favorite weapon of YHWH in the North to make his presence known (see 1 Kgs 13:24-32; 20:35-36).

The situation is reported to the king of Assyria by unnamed sources. These sources correctly identify the lions as divine retribution but do not identify YHWH as the god in question. Instead they say (twice!) that the inhabitants "do not know the rules of the god of the land" (v. 26). This generic reference suggests that the informers are meant to be Assyrian officials. To this report the king of Assyria responds directly, issuing an order that accepts the validity of the explanation, and offers an ironic solution to the problem. An unnamed priest among the exiles, deported because of their spurning of YHWH's laws, is now to be repatriated in order to teach the new inhabitants "the rules of the god of the land" (v. 27), the very same YHWH. Furthermore, the priest settles in Beth-el, the center of Jeroboam's cult of the molten calf, that the writer so condemns (e.g., v. 16). Of course, from the king of Assyria's point of view, it was his power, not YHWH's, that drove the Israelites from their land, so there is nothing ironic about sending back an Israelite priest. What is more, the remedy apparently works; no more is heard about the lions and the people learn how to "fear the LORD" (v. 28).

But if the priest's teachings successfully keep the lions at bay, they do not transform the settlers into exclusive worshipers of YHWH. Verses 29-33 describe in detail the syncretistic practices of the new inhabitants. Opening with a verb form indicating continuous, repetitive action and continuing with verbs in the perfect tense, the text identifies an ongoing situation that runs ahead of the narrative present. First, with more than a little sarcasm, the settlers, here termed "nations (*gôy*)," are said to have each "made (*ʿośîm*)" their gods, that is, constructed them. Having done so they deposit them in the *bamôt* that had been "made (*ʿośîm*)" by the Israelites, here termed "Samarians," a term that appears only here in the Bible. Not only do they create their own gods, but they worship them in the shrines earlier vilified by YHWH. Next, the gods are identified according to the nations that worshiped them and the nations are listed, with one exception, in the order in which they are introduced in v. 24. Several of the names of the gods are unknown from other Near Eastern sources (Succoth-Benoth, Adrammelech, and Anamelech), but the difficulties of historical identification should not prevent our noting the writer's aim to detail the deities of each of the nations that his source placed in the Assyrian province of Samaria. Indeed, even the abhorred practice of child sacrifice, for which the Israelites were condemned (v. 17), reappears in the cult of the Sepharvites (v. 31).

Verse 32 parallels v. 29 in its opening formulation: "And they continued (*wayyihĕyû*) to fear the LORD" recalls "And they continued (*wayyihĕyû*) to make each nation its own gods." Indeed the simultaneity of the two actions is brought out nicely in v. 33 in which reverse word order emphasizes the two equivalent direct objects of worship: "The LORD they were fearing and their own gods they were serving." They may have learned the "rules (*miśpaṭ*) of the god of the land" (v. 27), but they also follow the "rules *(mišpaṭ)* of the nations from which they were exiled" (v. 33). And the one priest sent by the king of Assyria did not suffice. At the same time that they worshiped YHWH they appointed their own priests to serve at the *bamôt* (v. 32). Until this point the writer refrains from directly evaluating the worship that he has described. The foreigners only do what comes naturally: they import their gods and cult from the old country and they worship YHWH as well.

The last section, vv. 34-41, moves from report to commentary, structurally equivalent to vv. 7-23. The last three words of v. 41, *ʿad hayyôm hazzeh* ("until today") repeat the first three words of v. 34, forming an inclusio bridging the chronological gap between past and present. Although v. 33 asserts that the settlers "feared the LORD," v. 34 states quite baldly that they did not. Now from his own perspective the narrator proceeds to critique the descendants of the settlers for persisting in the "first practices" of their ancestors. Now worship of YHWH is equated with obedience to the "laws, rules, teachings, and commandments" that YHWH had given to Israel. This is clearly a higher standard than they could ever be expected to follow. In fact, by indicating that YHWH had commanded all of these to "the sons of Jacob to which he gave the name Israel," the narrator would seem to be excluding the settlers and their descendants from even having received them, let alone being able to follow them. The writer invokes the voice of YHWH to deliver the heart of the Deuteronomic law that the inhabitants ignore: the prohibition of the worship of gods besides YHWH (vv. 35-39). Three times he says "do not worship other gods," and he stresses the loyalty owed to YHWH because of the covenant made with them. Of course, the covenant was not made with the current inhabitants of the land, so why criticize them for not adhering to it? The writer seems to assume that as inhabitants of YHWH's land, they can be held responsible for YHWH's covenant. The narrator follows YHWH's speech with a reprise of their fault: following the "first practices" of their ancestors (v. 40) and worshiping idols alongside of YHWH (v. 41). Lastly, the narrator takes his story into the present, accusing his contemporaries in the North of apostasy rooted in their ancestors' practices.

Part Four

RENEWAL AND CATASTROPHE FOR JUDAH
2 Kings 18–25

Chapter 24

HEZEKIAH'S REFORM, REBELLION, AND RECANTING

2 Kings 18:1-16

With a punctuating *wayĕhî* ("thus"), the royal chronicling resumes after the didactic explosion of chapter 17. Perhaps this opener signals that the report to be given about Hezekiah of Judah in vv. 3-7, will differ from those of his predecessors. Indeed, Hezekiah appears as the opposite of his father Ahaz. If Ahaz did not do what was right in YHWH's eyes as David had done (16:2), Hezekiah does. If Ahaz sacrificed and offered incense at the *bāmôt* (16:4), Hezekiah destroyed them. The emphatic "he" *(hû²)* and the subject-verb word order in v. 4 emphasize Hezekiah's personal responsibility for the destruction of the idolatrous cult in Judah. Four powerful verbs of destruction followed immediately by their direct objects express the writer's valorization of these violent acts: "He removed the *bāmôt*, shattered the pillars, cut down the asherah, and smashed the bronze serpent . . ." (v. 4). Along with the destruction of the bronze serpent comes an explanatory note linking the serpent to Moses and revealing the persistence of a form of worship instituted by Moses, but here chained to a series of idolatrous cultic loci justly destroyed by Hezekiah.

Following Hezekiah's lauded acts of destruction, the writer continues to praise Hezekiah for his fidelity to YHWH, employing two verbs never before predicated of the kings: *bāṭāḥ* ("he trusted," v. 5) and *wayyidbaq* ("he clung," v. 6). Indeed, to stress the contrast between Hezekiah's loyalty and that of his successors and predecessors, verse 5 begins with the direct object: "In the LORD the God of Israel he trusted." The claim of his singularity in comparison to those who came after him positions the writer in a time much later than Hezekiah himself. This superlative evaluation suggests that either the writer precedes Josiah, who is similarly praised (23:25), or he writes even later, say during the exile, but sees Hezekiah as greater than Josiah. In either case, the phrase that calls him more faithful than his predecessors, attached rather awkwardly to the verse, aims to exalt his fidelity above that of all other monarchs. Next his "clinging" to YHWH is explicated as his keeping of the commandments. Here the author invokes the name of Moses once again, this time to align Hezekiah with the positive tradition of obedience to YHWH's commandments rather than to repudiate the negative tradition of the worship of the bronze snake.

Verse 7 concludes the litany of praise with a theological interpretation of Hezekiah's successes as YHWH's response to his piety, here stated baldly as "The LORD was with him, and in everything that he went for he succeeded." Next we hear that Hezekiah revolted against the king of Assyria, the revolt thus marked as one of those successes. Indeed this announcement is followed in v. 8 with the report of Hezekiah's military triumphs against the Philistines. The importance of Hezekiah's role here is again conveyed by the emphatic, opening "he" *(hû²)*, and the completeness of this victory by the idiom of inclusion that ends the report: from watchtower to fortified city (the same phrase in 17:9 indicates the inclusiveness of Israel's idolatry expressed by the omnipresent erection of shrines). Interestingly, the announcement of Hezekiah's revolt against Assyria, which will bring about the main action, is sandwiched between the general statement of Hezekiah's success in everything and the specific example of his territorial expansion in Philistia.

A second report of Shalmaneser's conquest of the North (vv. 9-12) here fits within the historical framework of Hezekiah's reign and views that conquest in a more detached fashion. The beginning of the siege of Samaria is dated first to the fourth year of Hezekiah and then to the seventh year of Hoshea, while the capture of the city occurs three years later. Here the report is more matter-of-fact than in chapter 17. It does not mention Hoshea's treachery, imprisonment, and failure to pay tribute. That is all part of the story of the North, while from Judah's perspective, what matters is the siege and capture, and then the exile. Verse 11 repeats nearly verbatim 17:6, while v. 12 summarizes the theological indictment of 17:7-18 but in more precise Deuteronomic language: they didn't listen to the "voice" of YHWH; they transgressed "his covenant, all that Moses the servant of the LORD commanded." Moses was never mentioned by name in the lengthy harangue of chapter 17, but here the appearance of the name serves to contrast Israel with Hezekiah who *did* do all that Moses commanded.

Verse 13 picks up from v. 8, recording Assyria's reaction to Hezekiah's rebellion following Shalmaneser's capture of Samaria. Ten years later, the towns of Judah are attacked by Assyria. The same verb (ʿālāh, "went up against") conveys the parallel fates of Samaria and the Judahite towns. The voice of Hezekiah sounds for the first time: a plaintive, pleading voice knuckling under to the great Sennacherib. He whose obedience to YHWH is unmarred confesses that "I have sinned" to Sennacherib, and he begs to pay tribute. First naming the enormous sum that the king demands, the narrator then tells of Hezekiah's extraordinary efforts to raise it. Not only does he raid the temple and palace treasuries but he rips off the doors of the temple which he himself had had gilded. Hezekiah is shown capitulating to the full extent possible.

Chapter 25

THE FIRST ASSYRIAN MISSION TO HEZEKIAH AND ISAIAH'S ORACLES

2 Kings 18:17–19:9a

The narrator does not record any verbal response from the king of Assyria to Hezekiah's message and offer of tribute. Instead the narrative turns to an expansive dramatic enactment of the appearance of Sennacherib's official delegation to Jerusalem, its leader's crafty speech to Hezekiah's representatives, their report to Hezekiah, his appeal to the prophet Isaiah, and the prophet's response. Actually the text records two successive dramas with parallel, if unequal, elements (the second in 19:8-36). Bracketing the genetic questions, we may examine the effect of the juxtaposition and differing emphases of the two sequences. Thematically they clearly transform the political issue of Hezekiah's subordination into a nuanced discussion of weighty theological issues.

The delegations meet (18:17-18)

In two verses the text sets up the confrontation between the representatives of Sennacherib and those of Hezekiah. In lieu of a simple verbal answer to Hezekiah's obsequious offer (v. 14), comes a named delegation along with "strong troops" *(bĕḥêl kābēd)*. Even before they speak we know the news is not good. Had Sennacherib been satisfied with the tribute, he would not send his closest advisors. By naming the members of the delegation by their titles and not their names, each preceded by ʾet, the sign of the direct object, the narrator emphasizes the weightiness of these officials. And following their names the accompanying "strong troops" appear, completing the intimidating scene. Even the seemingly erroneous repetition of the verbs "and they went up and they came," followed the second time by "and they stood," contributes to hinting at the fear that they would inspire from the point of view of the Judeans. The names of the officials come from the Akkadian: Tartan meaning "viceroy," Rabsaris "chief eunuch," Rabshakeh "chief butler."[1] Still in the same verse the narrator specifies the location where the Assyrians take their stand. Though scholars may disagree about where exactly that location is, it is clear that the writer meant to specify a place known to his readers and thereby lend veracity to his report.

Verse 18 symmetrically names the three Judahite respondents to the Assyrians' summons, including proper names as well as titles. They too are high government officials. Like a description of a shoot-out in a Western movie, the scene depicts the two opposing sides facing each other. The naming of the negotiators brackets the specification of the meeting place.

The Rabshakeh's first address (18:19-25)

With the teams in place the high-level intimidation can begin. The Rabshakeh opens with a messenger formula calculated to impress the opposition: "Say now to Hezekiah, 'Thus the great king, the king of Assyria, says, "What is this security in which you have secured yourself?"'" By calling Hezekiah by name but omitting his title, the Rabshakeh implicitly denigrates the Judean king. At the same time, in referring to his own king he uses his title and epithet but not his name, thus elevating him. By claiming to report the king of Assyria's words to Hezekiah in the first person, the Rabshakeh minimizes the effect of intermediation, and we hear Sennacherib speaking directly to Hezekiah.

Sennacherib's reported words aim at undercutting the authority of Hezekiah by ridiculing the trust Hezekiah has placed in Egypt and in Yнwн. First he mocks Hezekiah's reliance on Egypt by hammering home the verb *baṭāḥ* five times in vv. 19-21: "What is the security *(biṭāḥôn)* on which you have relied *(bāṭāḥtā)?* . . . . On whom have you relied *(bāṭāḥtā)* that you have rebelled against me? Look, you have

---

[1] Mordechai Cogan and Hayim Tadmor, *II Kings,* Anchor Bible 11 (Garden City, NY: Doubleday, 1988) 229–230.

relied *(bāṭāḥtā)* upon a splintered reed . . . Thus is Pharaoh to all those
who rely *(habboṭḥîm)* upon him." That trust in Egypt is the object of the
Rabshakeh's scorn is not clear at the outset of the speech. Against the
background of the narrator's earlier praise of Hezekiah because "he
trusted *(baṭāḥ)* only in the LORD the God of Israel" (v. 5), we might expect Sennacherib first to ridicule this trust. Indeed, the Rabshakeh
withholds the mocked object of Hezekiah's trust, Egypt, until the last
moment: "Look, you have relied upon a splintered reed, this crushed
one, Egypt . . ." The delay builds suspense and the naming of Egypt
allows a momentary relief, since the Judahite emissaries can still have
confidence in YHWH.

But no sooner is the relief granted, than it is snatched away. The
Rabshakeh anticipates their response: "And if you say to me, in the
LORD our God we trust *(bāṭāḥnû)* . . ." (v. 22). The Rabshakeh's Sennacherib imagines the Judeans (the Hebrew verb "say" is in the plural
even though LXX and Isa 36:7 both read singular here) claiming to
trust in YHWH, so he then undercuts that claim by pointing out that
Hezekiah has destroyed the *bāmôt* and altars and demanded exclusive
worship in Jerusalem. Referring to Hezekiah in the third person (v. 22),
the Rabshakeh appeals directly to the emissaries before him and beyond them to the people on the wall—grandstanding, so to speak. By
quoting Hezekiah's demand for worship exclusively in Jerusalem, he
makes Hezekiah's reform out to be even more stringent than did the
narrator (v. 4). And he appeals to a common sense question: why destroy the altars of a god you claim to worship? Though in terms of textual history this may be a Deuteronomistic retrojection of conditions
after the Josian reformation, here against the background of the narrator's more limited description of Hezekiah's reformation, it serves to
exaggerate Hezekiah's reform for the purpose of raising doubts about
Hezekiah's devotion to YHWH.

In the voice of the Rabshakeh we most likely hear the voice of Judeans who opposed Hezekiah's reforms. Hezekiah's destruction of
provincial shrines would surely have had enormous economic and
religious repercussions upon the landholders and priests in the countryside. They would have seen in Hezekiah's actions the extirpation of
entirely appropriate worship of YHWH and could well have blamed
him for the catastrophe of the Assyrian invasion. By putting their ar-
guments in the mouth of the enemy, the writer demeans them.

In v. 23 the Rabshakeh speaks for himself, referring to his "master"
in the third person, and returning to the subject of foolish reliance on
Egypt. Offering a wager in the name of "my lord the king of Assyria,"
he claims the king is willing to give two thousand horses "if you can
provide yourself with riders for them." The Rabshakeh mocks Judah's

weakness, lampoons its inability to muster riders, and asks, in consequence, what Egypt can provide that Assyria cannot.

Finally, the Rabshakeh swings back to the theological track. Having undercut the popular image of Hezekiah's loyalty to YHWH, the Rabshakeh declares that it is really the king of Assyria who has been loyal to YHWH. "Without the LORD would I have come up against this place to destroy it?" he asks. "The LORD said to me, 'Go up against this land and destroy it!'" The Rabshakeh thus creates a stunning reversal of our expectations by questioning Hezekiah's loyalty to YHWH but claiming instead Sennacherib's. Reverse subject-verb order in v. 25b places YHWH in the first position to underscore the astounding claim that *YHWH* has spoken to the Assyrian king. The narrator has the Rabshakeh attribute to the king of Assyria the status of servant of YHWH that the narrator earlier claimed for Hezekiah. His double shift from political (Egypt) to theological (YHWH) questions leaves his Judahite opposites speechless. In this first speech the king of Assyria has argued that reliance on Egypt is worthless, questioned Hezekiah's loyalty to the god he claims to rely upon, and coopted this same god to justify his own conquest.

The Rabshakeh's second address (18:26-36)

The deep irony of the Rabshakeh's astounding proclamation that the king of Assyria destroys Judah at YHWH's behest at last causes the Judahite officials to break their silence in order to request that the Rabshakeh switch from the "Judean" language (i.e., Hebrew) to Aramaic, so that only the officials will understand his words. Suddenly the reader becomes aware of a heretofore unmentioned linguistic issue. Not only does the Rabshakeh usurp the native god YHWH for his own purposes, but he does so in the native language. Realizing that his insidious claims can be understood by the masses whose faith in Hezekiah and YHWH may, as a result, be undermined, the Judahite officials seek to keep communication on an official plane in the lingua franca, Aramaic. But the Rabshakeh scorns their appeal, making explicit what was already clear in his first address, that it is precisely to the common people that he speaks, those "sitting on the wall to eat their dung and drink their urine with you" (v. 26). Such is the fate of a city besieged by Assyria.

After this sharp exchange, the narrator introduces the Rabshakeh's second speech, addressed to the people as a whole, by specifying that he speaks "in a loud Judean voice" contravening the request of Eliakim (v. 28). Again he begins with a messenger formula, like a prophet introducing the word of YHWH: "Hear the word of the great king, the king of Assyria." The epithet "great" *(gādôl)* echoes the "loud" *(gādôl)* voice in which the Rabshakeh speaks. To this audience he does not begin with rhetorical questions but a series of commands. In three rapid negative imperatives (vv. 29-31a) he undercuts the authority of the Judahite king whom he repeatedly demeans by employing his name and not his title in contrast to his exclusive use of title to refer to the king of Assyria. In explaining these imperatives he flatly denies that, first, Hezekiah or, second, YHWH can save Jerusalem. But the level of authority ascends beyond YHWH to, in v. 31, the king of Assyria who alone has the power to save. The Rabshakeh's commands chart an ascending level of authority. In v. 29 he impugns Hezekiah's ability to save. The third command—"Do not listen to Hezekiah" (v. 31a)—issues in an extended promise by the king to whom Jerusalem *should* listen: Sennacherib.

Here the negative imperative pattern gives way to Sennacherib's seductive image of peacefulness and plenty. Having accused Hezekiah of beguiling his own people, it is ironic that beguilement is precisely Sennacherib's game and doubly ironic that that fulfillment is offered as the consequence of surrender. More ironic still is the Rabshakeh's use of stereotyped Israelite images of prosperity to describe those consequences. First, he evokes the golden age of Solomon, when safety meant "everyone under his own vine and under his own fig tree" (v. 31; cf. 1 Kgs 5:5), to characterize the immediate post-surrender peace. Then he makes exile attractive by attributing to the unspecified destination the standard Deuteronomic products of the land of Israel: grain, vineyards, bread, wine, oil, and honey (v. 32). This romanticized snapshot concludes with the Rabshakeh's repetition of the same negative imperative with which he opened—"Don't listen to Hezekiah!"—driving home the veracity of the alternative voice of Sennacherib that sounded between them.

Verse 32 concludes with a further repetition of the charge of Hezekiah's false assurance of YHWH's ability to save, but now the Rabshakeh offers evidence to back up Sennacherib's accusation that YHWH will not save Jerusalem. Appealing to history, he asks rhetorically which of the gods managed to save their peoples from the king of Assyria, naming a number of conquered nations and ending climactically with Samaria. While to the officials he spoke with the official Deuteronomistic theology that YHWH controls the fate of nations and thus, he says, summoned Sennacherib to destroy Judah, now to the people he articulates the popular view that each nation has its own god and YHWH is no different from any of them. If those gods have not saved, neither can YHWH! Like the officials earlier, now the people too are silent, in fact, have been silent, the verb form suggests (v. 36). Indeed now the narrator discloses that their silence was ordered by the king, an order they follow despite the Rabshakeh's provocation. The engagement with Sennacherib's challenge is left for the prophetic inquiry to follow.

Hezekiah turns to Isaiah (18:37-19:7)

Verse 37 begins a new scene as the narrative action resumes. Hezekiah's representatives, now named again, perhaps to underscore the official nature of their mission, report the Rabshakeh's words to the king. The narrator assumes Hezekiah's point of view; he is presumably in the palace out of earshot of the proceedings on the city wall, having left the negotiations to his subordinates. Thus we see the arrival of the officials through his eyes: "they came [not went] . . . with ripped garments." Before they can even speak their apparel signals a peril! The tearing of garments is a sign of mourning but also of serious repentance (e.g., 2 Kgs 6:30; 22:11). The narrator only reports their reporting; he wastes no time summarizing it. Instead he displays the reaction of King Hezekiah (pointedly here given his proper title, underscoring the blatant disrespect of the Rabshakeh's repeated references to him by name only): he too rips his garments and dons sackcloth (another sign of utter humility before God), and proceeds to the house of YHWH (19:1). He also sends his officials (replacing Joah with elder priests), properly suited in sackcloth, to the prophet Isaiah with a message reported, for maximum effect, not in its commissioning but in its delivery.

Hezekiah's message is at once reflective, direct, and pious. Beginning in a formal cadence he describes the current predicament as one shared by both Jerusalem and YHWH: "A day of distress, rebuke, and blasphemy this day is" (v. 3). He evokes the siege of Jerusalem but also alludes to the attack on YHWH by the Rabshakeh. He follows with what must have been a common proverb encapsulating the effects of a siege: "For children have come to the birthstool but the power to give birth is lacking." After this introduction he turns directly to the theological crisis spurred by the Rabshakeh's denial of YHWH's power to save, properly suggesting that "perhaps" (*ʾûlay*) YHWH has heard this attack and will respond with appropriate judgment. Hezekiah ignores the other elements of the Rabshakeh's address, appealing to YHWH only to defend his own honor against blasphemy. Thus in Hezekiah's message the struggle between the king of Assyria and Hezekiah is transformed into an Assyrian challenge of YHWH, the "living God" himself. Hezekiah addresses Isaiah as an intermediary who can turn to YHWH "your God" in prayer and intervene for the welfare of the present victims of the siege.

Isaiah's response is short and direct. Playing upon the verb *šāmaᶜ* (hear), Isaiah sets the rumor *(šĕmûᶜa)* that the king of Assyria will hear *(šāmaᶜ)* against the words that Hezekiah has heard *(šāmaᶜtā)* from Rab-shakeh (v. 7). YHWH's word will thus defeat that of the king of Assyria. Isaiah's oracle, furthermore, predicts the defeat of the king of Assyria by the sword in his own land. In all of this YHWH is in control: sending a rumor and bringing down the king.

At last there is some response to the word of the Rabshakeh. Heze-kiah's emissaries and the people on the wall all were silent in the face of the charges and insults brought by the Rabshakeh in the name of the king of Assyria, because the challenge needed to be handled on the proper plane. In response to the king of Assyria's theological interpre-tation of his success, that he is empowered by YHWH himself (18:25), who will not save Jerusalem (v. 32), only an alternative theological ex-planation will do, and that can come only from YHWH's prophet. Thus it is Isaiah who, in a brief oracle, accuses the king of Assyria of blas-phemy and predicts his downfall.

Meanwhile back at the front (19:8-9a)

Only now is the Rabshakeh's departure reported. Not until Isaiah has issued his oracle undercutting the Rabshakeh's words does he "re-turn." The effect of the delay in the reporting of the Rabshakeh's de-parture is to have him leave defeated, not triumphant. Even though the Rabshakeh does not hear Isaiah's oracle, we do. As a result when the Rabshakeh departs, confidence in YHWH is buoyed. Meanwhile the king of Assyria seems less in control: the Rabshakeh finds that he has left Lachish for Libnah where he is embattled, and he (whether Sen-nacherib or the Rabshakeh is not clear) also has heard *(wayyišmaᶜ)* that the king of Cush wants to take him on. The echo of the verb *šāmaᶜ* hints that the rumors that Isaiah predicted have already begun.

Chapter 26

THE SECOND ASSYRIAN MISSION
TO HEZEKIAH AND ISAIAH'S ORACLES

2 Kings 19:9b-37

A somewhat unusual Masoretic punctuation, a space break in the middle of a verse, divides v. 9 into two parts. The break signals the end of the battlefield report and the return to the main topic, a second deputation to Hezekiah in Jerusalem, this time by anonymous messengers. Without the elaborate staging of the first message or the histrionics of the Rabshakeh, this declaration from Sennacherib is not delivered orally but in written letters (*hassĕpārîm*, v. 14). And what takes up the most space in this narrative is the oracular response of Isaiah.

The Assyrian warning (19:9b-13)

This warning, consistently verbed in the second person singular, is directed to Hezekiah personally. Whereas the Rabshakeh warned the people against letting Hezekiah mislead them, this message warns Hezekiah against letting YHWH mislead him. The letter goes on to remind Hezekiah of what he has "heard" about all of the lands that the king of Assyria has utterly destroyed. "And you are going to escape?" it asks tauntingly (v. 11). This message focuses exclusively on Hezekiah's false hope that Jerusalem will be saved. It repeats the precedents of the Rabshakeh's second speech (18:34-35) and supplements them with even older examples of kings destroyed by Sennacherib's predecessors. The list of names of nations not saved by their gods is meant to strike at the base of Hezekiah's faith. Though YHWH here is not mentioned by name, the challenge is laid at his feet: if the other gods did not save their nations, how can you, Hezekiah, believe that your god will save Jerusalem?

135

Hezekiah's prayer (19:14-19)

Having, in response to the Rabshakeh's message, appealed to the prophet Isaiah for intermediation, Hezekiah now approaches Y<small>HWH</small> directly by "spreading out" the letter "before the L<small>ORD</small>" in the temple, in effect offering it to Y<small>HWH</small> for a response. In this setting Hezekiah's prayer to Y<small>HWH</small> rebuts the theological attack of the Assyrians and asks Y<small>HWH</small> to vindicate that rebuttal by saving Jerusalem. It is in form and content a masterful piece fit for a king whose faith receives such high marks by the Deuteronomist (18:5-6). The prayer begins with an apostrophe to Y<small>HWH</small> in his military mode: enthroned between the cherubim atop the Ark of the Covenant he was pictured marching out to battle with his "hosts." Then with an emphatic *ʾatāh* (you), Hezekiah proclaims Y<small>HWH</small> as the sole governor of all nations and sole creator of heaven and earth, effectively denying the Assyrian charge of Y<small>HWH</small>'s powerlessness.

Verse 16 turns from praise to petition, calling upon Y<small>HWH</small> to focus on the blasphemy of Sennacherib, referred to now by Hezekiah, with deserving condescension, by his name and *not* his title. Hezekiah's call to attention takes the form of two parallel imperatives—"Incline, L<small>ORD</small>, your ear and listen. Open, L<small>ORD</small>, your eyes and see"—followed by a third imperative directing Y<small>HWH</small>'s attention to the words of Sennacherib. Having spotlighted those words, Hezekiah next acknowledges the historical truth of Sennacherib's major claim, but undercuts the lesson Sennacherib derives from that claim. Thus while the Assyrians have destroyed the nations and their gods, these gods, he insists, were only human handiwork. The precedents that the Assyrians cite are no precedents at all, Hezekiah implies, for Y<small>HWH</small> is not wood and stone; he is the "living God." In the closing appeal Hezekiah begs for deliverance from Assyrian hands, so that the mockery of Sennacherib can be undone, and the exclusive divinity of Y<small>HWH</small> may be known. Hezekiah's prayer raises the stakes of salvation. The point becomes not merely the defeat of Assyria but the demonstration to "all the kingdoms of the earth" of the sole and universal power of Y<small>HWH</small>.

Isaiah Prophesies the Retreat of Assyria (19:20-34)

Though Hezekiah bypassed Isaiah in this second turning to Y<small>HWH</small> and offers up his own prayer, it is Isaiah who delivers Y<small>HWH</small>'s response. Without intervening narration Isaiah reports Y<small>HWH</small>'s answer, presented as against (*ʿal*) Sennacherib. That answer comes in the form of three prophecies: a long poem taunting Sennacherib (vv. 21b-28), a sign of hope for the Judahite survivors (vv. 29-31), and an oracle of salvation for Jerusalem (vv. 32-34).

Vv. 21b-28: Against Sennacherib

Three voices speak in this poem. The first is the city of Jerusalem whom the poet introduces personified as a young woman. Her inner attitude is first disclosed followed by a physical gesture expressing it. So she despises and shakes her head mockingly but also, perhaps, with feigned sorrow and commiseration.[2] Her scorn is expressed most forcefully in the rhythm and assonance of the description: *bāzāh lĕkā lāʿagāh lĕkā* ("she despises you, she mocks you"). When she speaks it is not to protest the siege she has suffered but rather to revile Sennacherib's attitude toward YHWH. In two rhetorical questions and in their answer the verb "blaspheme" (*ḥēraptā*) twice appears and Sennacherib is accused of "raising up" both his voice and his eyes against "the Holy One of Israel."

The voice of Sennacherib comes as an inner voice imagined and quoted by the "Maid Zion." He names his feats like a superhero using the emphatic "I" (*ʾanî*) and stressing the superlative: highest mountains, peaks of Lebanon, loftiest cedars, choicest cypresses, farthest outpost, densest forest, all the tributaries of the Nile. He brags about his conquests of the forests of Lebanon and the rivers of Egypt, nature's greatest fertile wonders. He has drunk "foreign waters" (v. 24) and survived. Maid Zion does not picture here his military conquests—we have heard enough of those—rather his claim to have tamed nature is the hubris that brings on YHWH's response.

YHWH's voice breaks in abruptly (v. 25) to trump Sennacherib's bragging rights and to identify himself as the real power behind him. Reminiscent of the divine voice in Second Isaiah, YHWH asks rhetorically if Sennacherib does not realize that his accomplishments are the result of YHWH's age-old plans and current fulfillment. He compares the survivors of conquered cities to grass that somehow makes it through the hot summer *khamsin* or rooftop grass that withers for lack of rooting. He does not refer directly to the exploits about which Sennacherib brags in the poem, rather he responds to the earlier boasts about the nations he destroyed. Finally YHWH affirms his knowledge of Sennacherib's movements (v. 27) and identifies Sennacherib's blustering

[2] So Cogan and Tadmor, *II Kings*, 237.

and braggadocio as the cause of Yhwh's revenge. He pictures the Assyrian king as a beast of burden with bit and hook.

Vv. 29-31: For the survivors

In this short prophecy Isaiah offers a sign for the survivors that foretells their fate. He promises that even though in the current year and in the year to come they will not plant grain but will eat what grows of itself, in the third year they will sow and plant again. (Here the Hebrew uses two different rare words to denote unplanted grain: *sāpîaḥ* appears only here, the parallel in Isa 37:30, and in Lev 25:5; and *sāḥîš* appears only here.) It is a picture of extraordinary fertility: planting vineyards and eating their fruit in the same year; striking roots below and producing boughs above. The prophecy closes with a rhythmic oracle promising survival of a remnant of Jerusalemites, thanks to Yhwh's zeal.

Vv. 32-34: For Jerusalem

The final prophecy promises that Jerusalem will not be taken. In four parallel clauses each beginning with the word "not" *(loʾ)*, Sennacherib's power to take the city is rendered null and void. The oracle denies that he will employ either arrow, or shield, or siege ramp. Instead, it repeats the last line of the first poem as a refrain: "By the way that he has come, by it shall he return" (v. 33, cf. v. 28). And the last clause, "he shall not enter this city," repeats the first clause of this oracle, providing it a frame. Finally an addendum (v. 34) states positively the implication of the negative clauses before it. It cites two motivations for Yhwh's defense of Jerusalem: his reputation, to which Hezekiah referred in his appeal, and David, a reference to the traditional promise to David that Jerusalem would stand forever.

The result (19:35-37)

The consequences were not long in coming. Emphasizing that the event he is about to report took place "that very night," the narrator quickly reports a *deus ex machina*, the miraculous deaths of the incredibly large Assyrian force camped outside Jerusalem. We see the result from the perspective of the Jerusalemites: "and they woke up early in the morning, and behold, dead corpses" (v. 35). The narration of Sennacherib's subsequent retreat employs a sequence of verbs ("he pulled out, and he went, and he dwelled") that parallels the sequence of verbs describing his emissaries' approach to Jerusalem ("and they went up, and they came, and they stood" [18:17]), thus forming an inclusio around the episodes of the siege. The last chapter in the story of Sennacherib, joined paratactically but not explicitly consequentially to the foregoing, is the murder of the king while he is praying to "his gods." The irony of the scene elicits no comment from our narrator who steps back and lets us relish the patricide of the wicked king in the presence of his own gods. How better to convey the hand of YHWH at work! The final clause records the succession of Esarhaddon with the standard formula for Israelite kings, thus implying finally that this succession is also sponsored by YHWH.

Chapter 27

HEZEKIAH'S ILLNESS AND ITS CONSEQUENCES

2 Kings 20:1-21

Reprieve for a dying king (20:1-11)

The episode concerning Hezekiah's illness and his miraculous recovery is the fourth and last instance in 1–2 Kings of a type-scene in
which a dying king seeks or receives an oracle from a prophet about
his fate. Jeroboam (1 Kings 14), Ahaziah (2 Kings 1), and Ben-hadad
(2 Kgs 8:7-15) all send inquiries about their illnesses through prophets
and all receive death sentences from YHWH. Each of these episodes
plays upon a common pattern, thus establishing, on the one hand, the
divine rhythm moving through history and, on the other, the uniqueness of each historical moment. Against the convention of the type-
scene, the particular emphases of each episode can be read. Indeed, the
first three "dying king" tales serve as historical and literary backdrops
for our episode, which veers more radically than they do from the
putative type-scene that stands behind them all.

The connective narration relates this episode most loosely to the
foregoing ("in those days") and informs without further explanation
that Hezekiah is "sick to death" or, as we might put it, on his death
bed. In the other versions of the type-scene the kings in this predicament next send for a prophet to inquire of YHWH (in the case of Ahaziah
of Israel, Baal-zebub) whether they will recover. In fact, the inquiry itself follows a standard pattern. But here Isaiah the prophet comes un-
bidden to the king with an oracle that Hezekiah did not request! All
messengers are eliminated and the king deals directly with the prophet,
underscoring the close relationship between them, unlike the antagonistic relationship of Hezekiah's predecessors.

Within the Hezekiah tales this third entrance of Isaiah also indicates the tight link between Hezekiah and YHWH. After the first delegation from Assyria, Hezekiah turned to Isaiah to pray for him (19:3-4). After the second delegation, Hezekiah offers his own prayer (19:14-19) and Isaiah responds for YHWH. Now Isaiah appears even before Hezekiah prays, bearing an oracle of doom from YHWH (20:1). Isaiah acts purely as messenger, but if his stock is reduced, Hezekiah's with YHWH is advanced. Unlike the cases of the Israelite kings, Jeroboam and Ahaziah, the death sentence here does not come from YHWH as retribution for royal apostasy. In the case of Hezekiah there is no implication of illness and death coming as punishment for sin. On the contrary, we have heard only of Hezekiah's righteousness.

This episode begins where the other dying king episodes end, with the transmission of the death sentence to the dying monarch. By placing the death sentence in the first verse, in his own words and then in those of YHWH, the narrator focuses our attention not on the transmission of the oracle, which is of great interest in the earlier versions of the type-scene, but rather on Hezekiah's reaction to it. Here we see how the righteous king reacts. Only this king responds with a prayer for mercy. Having earlier prayed on behalf of Jerusalem, he now turns his face to the wall and prays for himself. His brief prayer opens with the classic Deuteronomic imperative, "remember!" and continues with a self-description that would make any red-blooded Deuteronomist proud: "I have walked before you truthfully and wholeheartedly. What was good in your eyes I have done" (v. 3). And the narrator adds, if we needed to be convinced of his sincerity: "He cried a great cry." In the parallel Benhadad scene, it is the prophet Elisha who cries out because he sees the horrible consequences for Israel of the oracle he is delivering. Here, in contrast, Hezekiah emotes, hoping to avert the fate decreed for him.

Our episode now charts a path different from its parallel predecessors, for Hezekiah's prayer is answered. The immediacy of YHWH's response is indicated by the verb forms in the Hebrew perfect: "And so it was that Isaiah had not yet left the middle courtyard when the word of the LORD came to him saying, . . ." (v. 4). Before he even gets out of the palace area, a divine word turns him around. Because the oracle is recorded in its transmission to Isaiah, who is told to go back and recite it to Hezekiah, the status of the prophet is again reduced to that of a messenger. The diminishing of the prophet's independence here makes way for an oracle that praises the king and promises him healing.

The prophecy concerns itself first with the future of Hezekiah. Again the close tie between YHWH and this king is stressed, in this case by the almost tender way that YHWH speaks of and to Hezekiah. The title *něgîd ʿammî* ("prince of my people"), for example, which is absent in the version of the oracle which appears in the book of Isaiah (Isa 38:4), is an honorific harking back to Saul, David, and Solomon (and used in Kings infrequently afterwards) and connoting chosenness. Then too YHWH refers to himself as "the God of your father David," linking Hezekiah directly to the chosen founder of the dynasty. Five first person verbs—"I have heard . . . I have seen . . . I heal . . . I will add . . . I will save" (vv. 5-6)—express YHWH's reversal of his first oracle. In parallel clauses YHWH confirms that he has heard and seen what the reader has also heard and seen: the prayer and tears of Hezekiah. They have moved YHWH to promise healing to be marked by a visit to the temple "on the third day," a stereotypical phrase meaning a short span of time. But YHWH's promise to his chosen king goes beyond mere healing.

His assurance of fifteen extra years represents a most unusual projection of an individual life-span, a divine confirmation of the high status in which Hezekiah is held. This specification also enables us to close a timing gap opened by the vague dating of this episode to "in those days" (v. 1). If Hezekiah were to live fifteen more years and his reign lasted twenty-nine years (18:2), then we are to understand his illness as occurring during the fourteenth year of his reign, before Sennacherib's armies have retreated. This oracle, which concludes with the promise of salvation for Jerusalem, is thus of a piece with those that came in response to the Assyrian challenges in the previous chapter. In fact, YHWH's motivation for protecting the city, to preserve his own reputation and because of his promise to David (v. 6), repeats that of the earlier oracle (19:34). If, in the first version of the type scene, Jeroboam and his house were destroyed because he did not follow David's example, Hezekiah and his city will be saved because he did follow David's example. In both cases a royal illness provokes an oracle that affects the destiny of the state as a whole. Hezekiah's recovery carries with it the promise of the salvation of Jerusalem from Assyrian hands just as Abijah's death presaged the death of Jeroboam's house altogether (1 Kgs 14:12-14).

Following the oracle are two actions that carry forward the theme of recovery. In v. 7 Hezekiah asks for a cure for what is apparently the outward sign of his illness, called here *šĕḥîn*, a boil or inflammation. The cake of figs that Isaiah orders apparently had medicinal qualities and was used elsewhere in the ancient Near East for similar purposes. Applied to Hezekiah, it does the trick and the narrator reports, "he lived." In v. 8 Hezekiah requests a sign that he will be healed and, when given the choice of an easy or more difficult miracle, he chooses the latter, involving apparently the reversal of time by the shortening of a shadow. The prophet calls to YHWH and YHWH makes the miracle happen.

Critics have various difficulties with these two brief episodes. If Hezekiah is already healed in v. 7, why, in v. 8, does he request a sign that he will be healed? The fig cure, moreover, does not comport well with the character of Isaiah known from his book and is more reminiscent of the wonder-working Elisha. And the particular sign offered, a violation of natural law, is also jarring. In the book of Isaiah the fig cure does not precede the shadow sign which, instead, follows immediately after YHWH's promise of fifteen years for Hezekiah and salvation for Jerusalem (Isa 38:7). There, equally puzzlingly, Isaiah request figs to cure Hezekiah only after Hezekiah has already recovered (Isa 38:21). And only after that does Hezekiah ask for a sign that he will go up to the temple, a sign not granted. In short, the sequence in Isaiah displays no more apparent logic than that in 2 Kings 20.

But if we think of the two actions, not as strictly sequential but as parallel, we can see that they illustrate two different dimensions of healing. The figs, applied to the outward manifestation of Hezekiah's illness, provide physical healing. Yet if all that Hezekiah needed in order to be cured were figs, one wonders why it took divine intervention to save him. Clearly the text implies that Hezekiah's "sickness unto death" is more than merely a skin disease. Hezekiah's request for a sign betrays his psychological need for assurance that in the midst of the illness ravaging his body and the Assyrians ravaging his state, he will not only survive, but his city will too, and that he will live to see it for fifteen more years. The sign given on the public timepiece, the "dial of Ahaz" (v. 11), links the personal and political salvations that YHWH has promised. Since attitudes toward and treatment of the physical body often symbolize a culture's sense of the social body, the attention shown to the impact of Hezekiah's illness reflects the author's concern for the effects of Assyrian domination on the body politic.[3]

Adumbration of a dark future (20:12-19)

The last episode involving Hezekiah depicts a visit by the king of Babylon and a final prophecy of Isaiah that looks beyond Hezekiah's personal reprieve to the disaster looming ahead for Judah. The narrator stages the visit "at that time," during Hezekiah's illness and makes a sick call the ostensible motivation of the cumbersomely named king

---

[3] See the use of Mary Douglas's theory in T. R. Hobbs, *2 Kings*, Word Biblical Commentary (Waco: Word Books, 1985) 292.

of Babylon. Indeed he comes bearing "books *(sĕpārîm)*" and a gift. The word *sĕpārîm* likely refers to an official letter; the same word was used earlier to denote what Hezekiah received from the messengers from Assyria. It is ironic that just after Hezekiah is assured by YHWH that Jerusalem will not fall, the king of the nation that ultimately conquers Jerusalem appears bearing gifts.

Hezekiah's reaction, upon hearing of the envoys' appearance, is to offer them a tour of his treasures and his armory. The contents of the letter are not disclosed, nor does Hezekiah answer Isaiah's request to know "what did the men say?" (v. 14). So we are left to infer Merodach-Baladan's real motivation for coming and Hezekiah's for showing off "the silver, the gold, the spices, and the fragrant oil and his armory" (v. 13). Has the Babylonian king proposed an alliance that would depend upon the depth of Hezekiah's resources? Has he promised support for Hezekiah in the struggle against Assyria if Hezekiah will submit to him as a vassal? Or has he requested aid from Hezekiah to topple Assyria in the east? However historians may decide this issue, what is striking from a literary perspective is how the issue is evaded both by the narrator and by Hezekiah in his response to Isaiah. Hezekiah not only avoids relating his conversation with Merodach-Baladan; he also responds vaguely at first to Isaiah's question of the man's origin. "From a far country" he first replies, as if to say, "What business is this of yours?" Only afterwards does he add, "they come from Babylon." And in answer to the prophet's question of what they have seen, Hezekiah only repeats what the narrator has already said, in precisely the same words.

The Hezekiah that emerges from this strange little encounter is not the openly pious, sincerely repentant, follower of YHWH that we have seen heretofore. Despite the healing, the sign, and the oracle of deliverance, Hezekiah seems to knuckle under to the king of Babylon, exposing his treasures before him in a gesture of submission. As well, in response to Isaiah's oracle, one not requested by Hezekiah, the king appears only too ready to glory in his own safety with little regard to the future. When the Assyrian invaders prophesied doom for Jerusalem, Hezekiah was down on his knees praying to YHWH for deliverance. But now he does not pray at all; he only affirms Isaiah's words saying, "the word of the LORD that you have spoken is good" (v. 19). And the narrator reveals his interior voice, calculating that the prophecy of the destruction of Jerusalem in the days of his sons must mean "peace in our time." For this Hezekiah that is enough.

Considering that only a few verses earlier YHWH had promised to "protect this city for my sake and for the sake of my servant David" (v. 6), his promise now that everything in Hezekiah's palace and all of his sons will be carried off to Babylon comes as a stunning reversal. If he gave Hezekiah a reprieve from his death sentence, now he makes it clear that the dynasty is on artificial life support. The placement of the Babylonian embassy and of YHWH's oracle pulls the rug out from under the assurances given Hezekiah and point toward Judah's ultimate fate. In the midst of Judah's salvation, the author wants to signal the story's conclusion. Hezekiah's display of the royal treasures to the Babylonian king serves to trigger the divine declaration that all of this will be taken to Babylon. Even the most righteous king has evinced a moral failing in his seeming capitulation to a Babylonian request, and so he must live out his extra years with the knowledge that Judah too is living on borrowed time.

Conclusion to Hezekiah's reign (20:20-21)

The fifteen years of Hezekiah's life after his illness are nearly a blank. No dramatized scenes or even reports fill in the time. Only in the final summary does the narrator mention the engineering feat which brought water from outside the wall into the city, but the significance of the accomplishment is not noted. What is today called "Hezekiah's Tunnel" brought water from the Gihon spring to the Siloam pool inside the city walls, providing a permanent water source even in times of siege. No tour of the "city of David" today is complete without sloshing, candles in hand, through the knee-deep water of the tunnel, past the spot where archaeologists discovered an inscription recording the reaction of the builders of the tunnel as they tried to link up with their colleagues coming from the opposite direction. The Chronicler includes some more information about this marvelous construction (2 Chr 32:3-5, 30), but our author, as usual, is unimpressed by engineering and simply reports the work without comment.

Chapter 28

TWO DREADFUL KINGS

2 Kings 21:1-26

The reigns of Manasseh and his son Amon are summarized without a single event rising to scenic disclosure, without a single human character being given a voice. The narrator wields a heavy hand here revealing only typical behaviors, not specific occurrences, and editorializing on their significance without a shred of nuance. So eager is he to denigrate Manasseh that a reign of fifty-five years, by his account, passes without mention of political life, though such information was available, at least to the Chronicler (2 Chr 33:14). Wicked kings these, they form an interlude between the extended presentations of the careers of the two good kings of Judah: Hezekiah and Josiah.

Manasseh's apostasy (21:1-18)

Against the orderliness of the standard formulaic introduction to Manasseh's reign, that gives his age at succession, the length of his reign, and the name of his mother, the account of his misdeeds is all the more shocking. The phrase "and he did evil in the LORD's eyes" frames the account (vv. 2, 16) and, in slightly modified form, is repeated twice more within it (vv. 6, 15). In the first part (vv. 2-9) the writer lists the charges against the apostate king, and in the second part (vv. 10-15) YHWH delivers his judgment against him.

In his list of charges against Manasseh, the narrator repeatedly compares him to others who came before him. Verses 2 and 9, providing an inner frame for the litany, set the broadest context by charging him with *tôʿabot haggôyim,* the abominations of the pre-Israelite inhabitants of the land driven out by YHWH. In this context Manasseh's acts are presented as a reversion to a wickedness that repudiates the entire history of YHWH's relationship with Israel in its land. The writer sees the practices he will describe not as foreign imports, adoption of Assyrian ways (as some scholars have claimed Manasseh's innovations to be), but rather as autochthonous worship never totally eliminated. In this Deuteronomistic perspective we hear the echo of Moses's ancient warning from the other side of the Jordan against the *tôʿabot haggôyim* (Deut 18:9). Indeed, it is specific practices and religious intermediaries outlawed there (Deut 18:10-14) that Manasseh is charged with supporting (vv. 5-6).

If Manasseh's apostasy recalls the oldest sinners, it also violates the practice of the most recent monarch. From the nations driven out before Israel, the object of comparison shifts to Hezekiah, the mostly righteous father of Manasseh. In fact, in the same verse (v. 3), Manasseh is compared negatively to Hezekiah and as equal in wickedness to Ahab, who here takes the place of Jeroboam as the standard for Israelite apostasy. By rebuilding the destroyed high places, Manasseh reverses Hezekiah's centralization policy. By adding Baal and Asherah to the pantheon, he adopts practices associated with Ahab. And by worshiping the sun, moon, stars, and planets, he incorporates common west Semitic worship. The mention of Ahab, whose apostasy brought down his dynasty, lends an especially dark note to the description.

Several subsequent verses raise the level of apostasy by noting the placement of the altars to these various false deities in the house of YHWH himself (vv. 4, 5, 7). And twice these announcements are appended by quotations of divine promises against which Manasseh's acts particularly offend. In the first of these (v. 4), the narrator recalls YHWH's declaration: "In Jerusalem I will put my name," naming Jerusalem as the place unspecified in the repeated Deuteronomic promise (e.g., Deut 12:5; 14:23). The recollection underscores the contrariness of Manasseh: in the very place where YHWH put his name, Manasseh built altars to the host of heaven. In the second (v. 7), another report of what Manasseh put in the temple (here the sculptured Asherah) triggers a lengthy quotation that combines elements of both Mosaic and Davidic covenant traditions (e.g., Deut 12:5; 28:2; 2 Sam 7:10). YHWH's choice of Jerusalem as the permanent dwelling place of his "name" is joined to the conditional promise of the land in return for obedience to the commandments. But "foreverness" of YHWH's name in the house and in Jerusalem is undercut by the conditionality of the land-holding. After YHWH's saving of Jerusalem during the reign of Hezekiah, the writer here begins to prepare the way for the destruction of Jerusalem by placing in YHWH's mouth a speech that makes YHWH's promise to

David and Solomon conditional upon obedience to the Torah of Moses. Against both of these promises—and the names of David, Solomon, and Moses—Manasseh's apostasy in the temple is shown as monstrous. The use of quotations, fabricated or not, lends an objective, bookish quality to the writer's evaluation of Manasseh. There is no ambiguity, no room for extenuating circumstances here, no chance to hear Manasseh himself.

In the middle of the report of Manasseh's patronage of autochthonous false deities comes the list of forbidden intermediations (Deut 18:10-11) that he is charged with practicing along with child sacrifice or something akin to it (v. 6). Here the writer repeats the opening theme— "he did much to do evil in the eyes of the LORD"—and augments the charge with a stereotyped phrase indicating Manasseh's motivation: "to cause anger [to the LORD]." Again we are at the mercy of the narrator who supplies not only Manasseh's actions but also his motivation.

The conclusion to the charges (v. 9) begins with a direct response to the divine promise in v. 8 which lays responsibility for survival in the land on the people's obedience to *tôrāh*. Now, for the first time, apostasy is attributed to the people at large: "They did not heed." But the next clause shifts back to Manasseh as the primary cause, leading the people astray. And the charges close with a return to the opening comparison, now crediting the people with more evil than their predecessors in the land.

The indictment (v. 11) and the punishment that follows (vv. 12-14) are delivered not by a named prophet but "by the hand of his servants the prophets." It is as if the gravity of Manasseh's sin is too great for a single prophet to take on. Nor is the prophecy addressed to Manasseh in the second person; rather it concerns Judah and Jerusalem in the third person. The writer presents the prophecy as a second-hand report, transmitted by nameless prophets about a wicked king. The mode of delivery thus furthers the distanced presentation of this reign that allows for no dialogue or dramatized action.

The indictment is delivered in formal style beginning with *ya‘an* ("because") and naming the guilty party "Manasseh, king of Judah." Two charges are brought against him. He is first charged with committing the *tô‘abot* ("abominations") of the pre-Israelite inhabitants of the land, here called Amorites. This charge summarizes the substance of vv. 2-8. The second charge indicts Manasseh for making the people sin with his fetishes, the situation described in v. 9.

With the formal *lāken* ("therefore") the penalty begins, and YHWH's first word, *hinnēh* ("behold") shifts us to the divine vision of the future already underway. Interestingly, Manasseh is neither addressed nor described in the punishment. It is Jerusalem and Judah who are the objects of God's wrath. They are linked with Samaria and the house of Ahab, both symbols of total destruction. After the prophecies of salvation for Jerusalem given to Hezekiah, this vision of Jerusalem wiped clean like a plate turned upside down begins to prepare the way for the disaster ahead. And YHWH's threat to "cast off the remnant of my inheritance" (v. 14) contrasts with his promise to Hezekiah to preserve a remnant (19:31). Having gotten warmed up, YHWH finally lambasts his people for angering him not just currently, but since the exodus from Egypt (v. 15). This blast is delivered as a second formal indictment parallel to that against Manasseh (v. 11). Manasseh seems quite forgotten in the penalty phase, having served as the stimulus for an oracle directed against the people at large. In fact, the writer is sensitive to that silence, because he appends a third charge against Manasseh (v. 16): he is accused of murdering innocents, filling Jerusalem with blood "mouth to mouth." This hyperbolic image returns the focus to Manasseh's sins. After this last charge, the second charge, that Manasseh caused Judah to sin, is repeated (cf. v. 11), forming an inclusio around the indictment and punishment.

Even the regnal summary diverges from its formulaic language to recall that not only his deeds but also "the sins which he sinned" can be found in the Chronicles of the Kings of Judah. Despite his outstanding sinfulness, Manasseh meets with no reported personal or professional adversity. The narrator tells of his long reign and peaceful burial in a garden (of king Uzziah? Of someone else named Uzza?). If divine justice is to be maintained, we must understand the oracle against Judah as the displacement of YHWH's wrath against Manasseh who "made Judah to sin."

Amon son of Manasseh (21:19-26)

The brief two-year reign of Amon is described in a manner befitting its length. Crowned at age twenty-two, he would have been born when his father was forty-five. Of course, if the expression "pass[ing] his son through the fire" (21:6) is a euphemism for child sacrifice, the older sons who were spared this ritual may have fled the country altogether! What stands out in the account of his reign is the comparison to his father. Three times in two verses he is credited with following his father's lead, doing the evil his father did, walking in the path his father walked, and serving the fetishes his father served. He is even buried in the same garden as his father. He does nothing on his own: he is simply a short-lived continuation of his father.

Only his manner of death is different from his father's. No motivation is given for the conspiracy that brings him down, nor for the "people of the land *(ʿam-hāʾāreṣ)*" who kill the conspirators and put (young) Josiah on the throne. Yet it is the same "people of the land" who assisted in the enthronement of young (seven years old) Jehoash by destroying the temple of Baal, its altars, images, and priest, ending the illegitimate reign of Athaliah (2 Kgs 11:18). As the named subject of two verbs in the same verse—"struck down" and "enthroned"—the "people of the land" emerge as the source of power at the beginning of Josiah's reign.

Chapter 29

JOSIAH FINDS A SCROLL
AND ORDERS A REFORMATION

2 Kings 22:1-23:30

The reign of Josiah is the culmination of 2 Kings, in fact of the entire volume of 1–2 Kings. He, alone of all the kings, is never criticized. Even Hezekiah, whose opening rating places him above all the kings who came before and after him, is, nonetheless, implicitly chided for displaying his treasures to the king of Babylon and expressing self-centered sentiments. The reformation that Hezekiah initiates reflects key features of Deuteronomic legislation understood as given by Moses but awaits Josiah for implementation. Josiah also holds the distinction of being the only king predicted by name long before his time (1 Kgs 13:2). The oracle of the old prophet from Judah, which promises that Josiah will desecrate the Beth-el altar, sends forth a prophetic trajectory at the outset of the history of the separate kingdom of Judah not fulfilled until now (23:16-18), nearly at the end of Judah's history.

The account of Josiah's reign is also key for source critics who overwhelmingly hypothesize that the scroll found by the high priest Hilkiah, on the basis of which Josiah orders his reforms, was at least the core of what became Deuteronomy. There are problems with this hypothesis, not the least of which is that the "found scroll" appears to be a literary *topos* not to be taken quite literally. Yet the affinity between Josiah's reforms (and to a lesser extent those of Hezekiah) and the most distinctive features of Deuteronomy is palpable. Whether the written source of Josiah's actions was "found" or fabricated, it must have included central elements that became incorporated in Deuteronomy.

Introduction to Josiah (22:1-2)

Compared to the narrator's build-up for Hezekiah, his introduction to Josiah is quite modest. After only one verse of praise, we are taken directly to the eighteenth year of his reign. In that verse (v. 2) Josiah is lavished with the same encomium granted to Hezekiah—pleasing to YHWH and following in the ways of David—and then credited with a Deuteronomic virtue (e.g., Deut 5:29; 17:11, 20; 28:14) not attributed to any other kings: "he did not turn to the right or to the left." Perhaps this initial matching of the two kings and then the brief deviation singling out Josiah is meant to signal that Josiah will not fall prey to weakness like Hezekiah. While Hezekiah's introduction continues with generous credits, the rest of the formulaic praise of Josiah is reserved for the conclusion at the end of his reign (23:25). Josiah thus ends as he begins, the fair-haired king who can do no wrong, while Hezekiah's dalliance with the Babylonian king has darkened his record which, at its conclusion, does not have a good word left for him.

Repairing the temple leads to finding a scroll (22:3-13)

All of the action recorded in Josiah's reign takes place in his eighteenth year when he would have been twenty-six years old. Having, like Jehoash before him, become king as a child (Jehoash was seven years old, cf. 2 Kgs 12:1), Josiah is not credited with independent action during his early years. But when he does act, his move is nearly identical to that of the earlier child-king: he attends to repairs of the temple (cf. 12:10-16). Again the money for the repairs is to be given to the "overseers of the work in charge of the House of the LORD" who will give it to the various tradesmen (vv. 5-6; cf. 12:12-13). Again the problem is the cracks in the temple *(bedeq habbāyit).* Again the workmen are listed and hewn stones are specified. Josiah here orders what the narrator reports to have been the case in the Jehoash story, that no concern be taken for those who oversee the delivery of the money, for they are honest. In fact, Josiah's speech is virtually a précis of the narrator's description of Jehoash's reform.

This repetition creates a kind of type-scene, a familiar context in which the surprise discovery of the scroll can have its maximum effect. Indeed, the entire order for the repair of the temple, though conveyed in the words of King Josiah, is subordinated to the finding of the scroll. "And it was in the eighteenth year of King Josiah, *when* the king had sent *(šālaḥ)* Shaphan son of Azaliah son of Meshullam to the house of the LORD saying, 'Go to the high priest . . .' (v. 3) . . . that Hilkiah the high priest *said (wayyᵓomer)* to the scribe Shaphan, 'A scroll of the Torah I have found . . .'" (v. 8). Thus the main verb in the sentence is "said," the order for the temple repair serving only as the backdrop. As well, Hilkiah's official title, "high priest," is included with his announcement in v. 8 as if he is being introduced for the first time, even though it has already been given in v. 4. The carrying out of Josiah's order and its transmission to Hilkiah are skipped over, opening a gap to be filled a bit later. For now Hilkiah's announcement takes center stage.

The writer emphasizes the significance of the discovery in several ways. First, Hilkiah's announcement reverses normal word order by leading with the direct object, focusing attention on it: "A scroll of the Torah I have found in the house of the LORD" (v. 8). Second, the importance of the find is measured by the speed with which the narrator reports still in the same verse that "Hilkiah gave the scroll to Shaphan and he read it." And immediately, "Shaphan brought the scroll to the king and brought back a message to the king" (v. 10). In contrast to Josiah's order to repair the temple, detailed in the commissioning but not the delivery, here every step of the transmission of the news is chronicled.

Third, Shaphan's relay of information to the king is designed to elicit the maximum response. Reversing the narrator's order of "bringing," Shaphan first reports on the mission on which the king had sent him and only afterwards mentions the scroll. Now the earlier gap is filled as Shaphan reports that the initial phases of the order have been carried out, the silver melted and given to the overseers to supervise the work (v. 9). Understandably the payouts to the various laborers and craftsmen have not yet occurred and so are not reported. With this information out of the way, Shaphan turns to the momentous discovery. Without indicating a specific response from Josiah to Shaphan's report, the narrator introduces the second part of Shaphan's speech with a new stage direction in v. 10, setting it off from the business of the day. Like Hilkiah, Shaphan begins with the direct object, springing the announcement on the king without any context, simply: "'A scroll Hilkiah the priest gave to me,' and Shaphan read it before the king." He does not identify what it is or where it was found; instead he gets right to the reading of it. By withholding the announcement of the scroll until after reporting on the status of the temple repair plan, he makes the announcement climactic.

Josiah's first reaction is physical, not verbal. In an interscenic summary, the narrator shows us the king hearing the words of the scroll (which is only now, as Josiah hears it, denominated specifically as a scroll of the Torah) and ripping his clothes. This behavior, expressive of repentance, also functions proleptically, pointing to a further reaction. That reaction is not long in coming. No sooner does he hear the scroll than he commands five of his trusted officials, including Hilkiah,

Shaphan, and Shaphan's son, to initiate a prophetic inquiry. The delegation is indicated by the specification of names and titles, signifying both
the official nature of the request and the importance that the king at-
taches to it. Indeed, the delegation is asked to inquire of YHWH not only
on behalf of the king but, in his words, "on my behalf, on behalf of the
people, and on behalf of all Judah." And they are to inquire about "this
found scroll." Like Shaphan, Josiah does not term it a scroll of the Teaching, a *sēper hattôrāh*, but rather "this found scroll," because its identity as
tôrāh has not yet been established. Although in his commission to the
delegation, he explains that YHWH's wrath must burn "against us because our fathers did not listen to the words of this book," (v. 14) he
nonetheless wants it verified by an official prophetic source before acting on it. Josiah's reaction seems to be largely one of shock conveyed by
his reasoning: if this found scroll is authentic, then YHWH's wrath must
be kindled because "our fathers have not done according to everything
written down for us" (v. 13). In this character-elevated scene, both Josiah
and Shaphan know the contents of the scroll, so far denied to the reader.
We know only that it prescribes behavior that "our fathers have not
done." For now we are kept in suspense about what that behavior is.

Huldah's oracle (22:14-20)

Repeating the names of the delegation of prophetic inquiry, the
narrator this time omits titles and genealogy. Though he calls no special attention to the fact that they head to a female prophet, he does
identify Huldah not by her own ancestry but by that of her husband.
Her oracle, issued on demand, has two parts, one concerning Jerusalem in general (vv. 15-17) and one directed at the king in particular (vv.
18-20). Both are carefully framed as the words of YHWH, spoken by
Huldah, reported by the narrator ("She said to them, 'Thus said the
LORD, God of Israel, Say to the man . . . Thus said the LORD, Behold I
am bringing . . . .'").

With the interjection *hinĕnî* ("behold") the first part of the oracle
shifts us to the divine point of view (v. 16). It begins with a confirmation of the scroll's words as YHWH's words and of the disaster at which
Josiah had hinted. More precisely, YHWH promises that evil will fall on
"this place and on its inhabitants" (v. 16). Only after he announces un-
conditional doom does he specify the reason for it: apostasy depicted
as betrayal of YHWH (v. 17). YHWH here speaks in personal terms: the
people angered him with their behavior, so he will take out his wrath
on them. Here YHWH accuses the people of the same deeds attributed

to Manasseh by the narrator (21:6). And he confirms, in the same words that Josiah uses, that "my anger is kindled *(niṣṣtāh ḥamātî),*" but adds that "it will not be quenched" (v. 17, cf. v. 13).

The second part of the oracle begins when Huldah breaks in with her own voice directing the divine words to "the king who sent you to inquire of the LORD" (v. 18). Although the oracle against Jerusalem was very vague, the protection offered Josiah is quite specific. Now we hear from YHWH's point of view a confirmation of the piety and sincerity of the king with which the narrator had opened his reign. In v. 19 YHWH reads Josiah's inner motivation ("your heart was softened and you humbled yourself") and notes his outward behavior ("you tore your clothes and cried before me"). Between those two observations YHWH reveals broadly what the scroll said to elicit that behavior, that both Jerusalem and its inhabitants will become "a desolation and a curse." The words of YHWH and the words of the scroll merge together as YHWH affirms that its words are his.

The oracle ends with YHWH's remarkable promise of personal salvation for Josiah. "Yes, I have heard," YHWH says dramatically after describing Josiah's penitent reaction upon hearing the curses of the scroll. As a consequence he assures him a peaceful death before the curses take effect. Verse 20 gives the consequence that follows upon Josiah's behavior. YHWH speaks directly to Josiah in the second person in vv. 18-20, remarkably excepting him from the fate he promises for the city and its people. The last clause in v. 20, "and they brought back word to the king," rounds out the delegation's mission and puts the ball back in the court of the king.

Josiah cuts a covenant (23:1-3)

Josiah's strength is implied by his reaction to Huldah's oracle of doom. He does not bemoan the fate of his people, nor does he ignore it, because he has been told that he will not have to live to see it. Rather he takes direct action just as he did upon first hearing the words of the scroll. He is the subject of all verbs in this section except the last (by which the people join into the covenant that he has proclaimed): he sent, gathered, ascended, read, stood, cut—a flurry of activity. In fact, the repetition of the verb "gathered" *(wayyeʾesôp* [reading with the parallel 2 Chr 34:29], cf. 22:20) links Josiah's action to his own ultimate fate as if to say that before he is "gathered to his fathers," he "gathers" his people to try to redirect them to YHWH. The text also stresses the inclusiveness of his assembly. The word "all" is repeated five times in two verses: all the elders, all Judahites, all Jerusalemites, all the people, all the words. Moreover, the phrase, "from the youngest to the oldest" (v. 2) denominates the whole population by age.

But though we are shown the various groups of people assembled, we *hear* nothing. The narrator now reveals yet one more feature of the mysterious scroll, by labeling it a "scroll of the covenant" and preparing us for the ceremony that Josiah so rapidly performs. Yet its contents are still not revealed; the writer maintains the suspense he created in the earlier readings of the scroll. Even though we are told that "all the words of the covenant scroll" are read, we hear not one. The covenant ceremony is described in silence without speech or dialogue. Instead we get in free indirect discourse the pledge that Josiah requires of the people: "to follow the LORD and to keep his commandments, his testimonies, and his statutes with all their heart and soul, to establish the words of this covenant written in this book" (v. 3). Here the king's summons and the people's response meld together without any clear attribution of the words to either one. And the people's one action— "they stood *(wayyaʿamod)* in the covenant"—is expressed by an unusual verb in this context, and so, does not offer a clear picture. So the covenant agreement entered into by the people precedes the reader's knowledge of what the stipulations of that covenant are.

Reforms in Jerusalem and Judah (23:4-14)

We learn the content of the covenant not by hearing a recitation of commandments, injunctions, and laws, but by watching the radical reformation undertaken by Josiah in the wake of its proclamation. Actually it is still not the content of the covenant that is revealed, only those flash points where its stipulations come into conflict with current practice. On that basis we can infer that the two foci of the covenant are the exclusive worship of YHWH exclusively in Jerusalem and the proper offering of the *pesaḥ*, the Passover sacrifice. Surely the covenant must have included more than this; indeed, most critics understand the covenant scroll to have been at least the core of what we know as the book of Deuteronomy. But our writer is clearly more interested in describing Josiah's cultic coup than in detailing the covenant contents.

Several features of this description stand out. First, King Josiah is depicted to be totally in control of the cultic purge that he orders. He is both sole author and sole actor. He is the subject of every verb of destruction; he is shown carrying out the reformation nearly by himself. Second, the verbs themselves are strong, pungent, and varied, and express the enthusiasm of the writer for the acts he describes. The litany of violence carried by these verbs produces a cathartic effect: idolatry in all of its forms is spewed out. In some verses sequences of action follow aspects of the reform to their completion (e.g., v. 6). Third, the writer makes liberal use of proper names—of gods, locations, kings—and particular objects. While the exact meaning of some of these eludes us, together they bespeak the effort to detail the revolution, to show how Josiah left no stone unturned in his destruction of offending cultic sites and practices. Finally, here too there are no words spoken: watching Josiah at work is like viewing a silent film clip of a pogrom. The lack of dialogue conveys the speed and efficiency with which Josiah wrecks the nativist cult without meeting a shred of resistance.

Although the account of Josiah's carnage seems somewhat random, one can perceive a rather general order to his deeds. Verses 4-7 focus on the destruction of idolatrous worship in the house of Yhwh in Jerusalem and in Judah. The names of the gods Baal and Asherah figure prominently in this section as well as the more generalized "host of heaven." All of the equipment (v. 4), personnel (vv. 5, 7) and images (v. 6) connected to the cults of these gods are removed and the objects destroyed. Much is made here of the totality of destruction with burning in the Kidron valley and scattering of ashes or dust twice mentioned. In the case of the "idolatrous priests" *(hakkĕmārîm)* and the "male prostitutes" *(haqqĕdēšîm)* not destruction but suppression seems to suffice. Both are fairly rare terms but clearly linked to a non-Yahwistic cult.[4]

In vv. 8-11 the focus shifts from the cults of other gods to that of Yhwh himself and from inside the temple to outside, first in Judah generally and then in Jerusalem. We first take a quick excursion to the countryside to witness the removal of the priests of Yhwh *(kohanîm)* from the rural shrines and the destruction of those shrines. The geographical note, "from Geba to Beersheba," indicates the inclusive range of the destruction in Judah from North to South. The mention of city-gate shrines, in particular one named after an otherwise unknown city governor Joshua, brings to our attention both a cultic location and a person otherwise unknown. If the reference is to Beersheba rather than to Jerusalem, the note would at least make better geographic sense and also explain the lack of other reference to it.[5] Verse 9 deals with the fate of the defrocked priests but in another not altogether clear way, though it appears that the point is that as unemployed *kohanîm*, they remained in the countryside with their fellow rustics rather than joining the Jerusalem priests. Verse 10 refers to

---

[4] *hakkĕmārîm:* Zeph 1:4; Hos 4:4; *haqqĕdēšîm:* 1 Kgs 15:12.
[5] Cogan and Tadmor, *II Kings,* 287.

the defilement of an apparently infamous shrine, named with the definite article *(hattopet),* used for some form of child sacrifice in a valley just west of Jerusalem.

What vv. 11-14 have in common is name-dropping, the attribution to specific kings of altars, shrines, and their accoutrements that are destroyed. In four verses contributions to apostasy by Kings Ahaz, Manasseh, and Solomon, as well as the "kings of Judah" in general are detailed, only to be removed, burned, torn, cut down, shattered, or scattered. At the same time the various locations of these sancta around Jerusalem are named, as are the gods Ashtoreth, Chemosh, and Milcom whose cults Solomon is said to have supported. Verses 12-13, repeatedly leading off with direct objects (e.g., "And the altars on the roof of the Ahaz upper room . . . the king tore down" [v. 13]), focus attention on the number of shrines to be destroyed as the reader anticipates the verb that will dispatch them. The clear message conveyed by the variety of verbs of destruction, the naming of the royal patrons associated with the now forbidden sancta, and the pulverization and desecration of the sites of apostasy is that Josiah's reform was complete and irreversible.

Reforms in the North (23:15-20)

From Jerusalem, the narrator's and Josiah's attention turn northward, first to Beth-el. What begins as a kind of addendum, in which the altar and shrine at Beth-el (v. 15) meet the same fate as those around Jerusalem (vv. 13-14), triggers an account of the fulfillment of an ancient prophecy (vv. 16-18) and the extension of Josiah's reform to all of the *bamôt* in Samaria, the Assyrian province formerly the northern kingdom of Israel. Interestingly, the text makes no reference to the foreign cult sites set up by the immigrants settled in Samaria by the Assyrians (17:29-32) and which were said to exist "to this day" (17:34, 41). Instead the text focuses only on those shrines built by the kings of Israel (vv. 15, 19) as if Samaria were an occupied territory of Judah rather than a foreign province.

Imitating the syntax of the verses concerning the destruction of the Solomon-sponsored shrines around Jerusalem (v. 13), the opening verse concerning Beth-el leads with the direct object and a long identifier before the verb is sounded: "And also the altar which was at Beth-el—the shrine which Jeroboam son of Nebat made who caused Israel to sin— and also that very altar and the shrine he *ripped down.*" The repeated conjunction *gam* ("also") links this destruction to the earlier ones as does the identification of the shrine with another king, the archetypal

Jeroboam. But here instead of shattering and cutting down, we get burning and beating of the shrine to dust.

In v. 16 Josiah is mentioned by name for the first time since 22:3. The narrator's litany of destruction is interrupted by the first staged scene since the beginning of the reform. Adopting Josiah's point of view, the narrator has him turn and see the graves on the hillside, and we see them along with him. As in v. 14 he uses human bones for the purposes of desecration, though this time he burns them on the remaining altar rather than scattering them over the destroyed sancta. We next discover that Josiah, by profaning the altar, has unwittingly fulfilled an ancient prophecy here referred to by the narrator. The reference is to 1 Kgs 13:1-2, the tale of the man of God from Judah who, in a *vaticinium post eventum* prophecy, mentions Josiah by name as the descendant of David who will burn bones on the altar of Jeroboam at Beth-El. A trajectory of expectation opened at the very beginning of the divided kingdom and arching over its history ever since here culminates in Josiah's action. The final stage in God's judgment against the northern secessionists, announced at the very beginning of Jeroboam's reign by the man of God from Judah, is here executed by the king soon to be praised as the best of the Davidides.

From our reader-elevated position, we witness the dialogue between Josiah and the unnamed men of the town (vv. 17-18). Innocently Josiah asks the locals, "What is this marker that I see?" They reply by recalling for Josiah the prophecy to which the narrator has already referred the reader and identifying the grave quite specifically as that of "the man of God who came from Judah." Immediately convinced of the truth of this report, he commands that the bones be allowed to escape the general exhumation and burning. His order, "Let him rest!," permits the only rest he allows in this chapter, since the man of God's remains are the only ones that survive the search and destroy mission. Further linking Josiah's encounter at the grave with the ancient prophecy, the narrator recalls the story of the old prophet from Beth-el (here referred to by the general provincial designation of Samaria) who asked to be buried beside the man of God from Judah (1 Kgs 13:31-32), and indicates that his bones too were undisturbed. As the old prophet acknowledged the validity of the man of God's prophecy when he buried him, now the bones of the man of God cast their protective power over those of the prophet's when the prophecy is at last fulfilled.

After this brief scenic respite from the litany of destruction, the carnage resumes in v. 19 with a general summary of Josiah's abolition of the *bamôt* in all the cities of Samaria, attributing them to the kings of Israel just as the southern cult sites were credited to the kings of Judah. Unlike the priests of outlying shrines of Judah who were brought to

Jerusalem, the priests of the northern *bamôt* are simply slaughtered—on the altars where they performed sacrifices, no less. Although the narrator does not refer us back to the prophecy of the man of God from Judah, this mass slaughter indeed conforms to that prediction (1 Kgs 13:2). The last clause, "and he returned to Jerusalem," marks the end of the reform in the North.

The consummation of the reform (23:21-25)

Josiah's final act is one not of destruction but of establishment. Paralleling in form the report of his initial order launching the war against alien cults, his directive to observe Passover ("and the king commanded *[wayeṣaw]*" [v. 21, cf. v. 4]) ends the reform on a positive note. Unlike the earlier command related as narration and directed to Hilkiah, the priests and the guards, however, this one appears as a direct address to the people as a whole. Josiah, who as the sole subject of all of the verbs of destruction is credited with single-handedly executing the reform, now turns to "all the people" for their contribution to the new era he has begun. This singular appeal to the populace underscores the significance of this observance in "the scroll of the covenant" again cited specifically as the source of the reform. Before the writer confirms that the king's command was obeyed (v. 23), he offers a long historical perspective on the event, glancing back to the time of the judges and across the monarchies of Israel and Judah to claim that no Passover "like this" had ever been observed in all those years. Several scholars argue that the uniqueness to which the text points is not the observance of Passover itself, but rather the mode of observance ("that kind of Passover" [vv. 22, 23]), according to the Deuteronomic legislation. They point to the Chronicler's account of Passover during the reign of Hezekiah (2 Chr 30:1-27) as a parade example of a pre-Josian Passover. But perhaps the account of Hezekiah's Passover is in accord with the larger role given to the earlier king in Chronicles; there Hezekiah scoops Josiah as restorer of what had become for its authors the primary annual festival. In any case, this historical perspective, along with its geographical sweep embracing both Israel and Judah, clearly sets Josiah's Passover as a unique and climactic event within the Deuteronomist's entire story. Verse 23 confirms that this Passover was celebrated for the first time in Josiah's eighteenth year, the same year in which the reform began (22:3).

Beginning with the conjunction "and also *(wĕgam)*," v. 24 announces itself as an addendum to an account that has already reached its end. From observance of Passover, the text veers to one more act of abolition. Like earlier series of objects of destruction (e.g., vv. 15, 19), here the targets—the practitioners of the occult and the objects of their worship—precede the verb. Josiah is again the subject of the verb, a somewhat figurative use of the verb "to burn," here carrying the sense of "ridding" in keeping with Deuteronomy's abhorrence of such practices (e.g., Deut 18:10-12). This additional act of religious fanaticism, though seemingly misplaced here, serves as the lead-in to the concluding justification of the reform in the second half of the verse: the demands of the scroll found in the Temple. The conclusion, reiterating the main points of the amazing story—the scroll, the place, the finding, the priest—finishes the narration of Josiah's reformation.

The accolades accorded Josiah preceding the formulaic conclusion of his reign ring an interesting variation on the equivalent description of his royal ancestor Hezekiah. The evaluation of Josiah establishes his superiority to all other kings, first comparing him to those who preceded him and then to those who followed him. The evaluation of Hezekiah works the comparison in the opposite order and comes at the beginning of the account of his reign rather than at the end (18:5), as here with Josiah. In both cases, though, the plaudits follow the account of the king's reformation. In the case of Hezekiah, the reformation occupies only one verse (18:4), the story of his reign focusing instead on the encounter with the Rabshakeh. But since the story of Josiah's reform is the only subject in the account of his reign, the evaluation comes here, at its conclusion. As well, while Hezekiah's superlative rating is based on his adherence to the "commandments that the LORD had given to Moses" (18:6), Josiah's is attributed in the very language of Deuteronomy ("he returned with all his heart and all his soul and all his might" [cf., Deut 6:5]) specifically to his return to "the whole Torah of Moses." Thus the writer carries through the theme of Josiah's reign.

The equally unique status given to both Hezekiah and Josiah creates a clear contradiction when 2 Kings is read continuously: they cannot both be superior to each other. A source critic might resolve the contradiction by attributing the description of Hezekiah to a writer who lived before Josiah and whose judgment was simply not deleted when a post-Josian writer made Josiah the acme of faithful royalty. Yet the Josian version flows more smoothly than the Hezekian and so suggests its prior origin. It reads chiastically: "Like him there was no one before him . . . after him there was no one like him." In the description of Hezekiah, on the other hand, the phrase "and those who were before him" is tacked on to an already complete sentence ("and after him there was no one like him of all the kings of Judah" [18:5]). The text offers no easy resolution of the contradiction; perhaps the greatness of both kings is the point and the stereotyped description ought not to be taken too literally.

God's wrath against Judah (23:26-27)

Interrupting the close of Josiah's reign, the voice of YHWH announces the ultimate demise of Judah. Lest we be buoyed by the rosy evaluation of Josiah, this announcement jolts us back to the reality that lies ahead. The repetition of the verb "turned back" establishes this interruption as a direct response to the praise of Josiah. Josiah "turned back to the LORD" (v. 25), "but the LORD did not turn back from his fierce anger" (v. 26). Josiah's fidelity, in other words, does not cancel out Manasseh's infidelity. The writer supports his contention by introducing the voice of YHWH, not heard since issuing his reprieve to Josiah through the prophet Huldah (22:16-20). Now he speaks again, not to anyone in particular and thus directly to the reader, justifying the destruction of Judah and Jerusalem despite the reform led by the most faithful king ever. Using specific Deuteronomic phraseology, YHWH identifies Jerusalem as the chosen city "where I said my name would abide." Thus on the heels of the praise of Josiah, the reminder of the sins of Manasseh sets the stage for the final act.

Conclusion of Josiah's reign (23:28-30)

The formulaic reference to the other deeds of Josiah's reign does not prepare us for the surprise two-verse account of Josiah's death at the hand of Pharaoh Neco at Megiddo. The full background is not given, although it sounds as if Josiah miscalculated how he would be received by Neco. The phrase "and the king, Josiah, went to meet him *(liqrāʾtô)*" (v. 29) is nicely ambiguous. Did he go to confront him, to stop him, or to negotiate with him? Showing no interest in the content of the meeting, the writer reports only that "he killed him at Megiddo when he saw him." More focus is placed on the proper transport of the body to Jerusalem and burial in the family tomb. The "people of the land" *(ʿam hāʾāreṣ)* are again named as the group that installs his son Jehoahaz as king just as they put Josiah on the throne after the conspiracy of his father Amon's courtiers against him.

Chapter 30

THE LAST FOUR KINGS OF JUDAH

2 Kings 23:31–25:7

Josiah's reign functions as the climax of 2 Kings. For the writer, be he pre-exilic or exilic, Josiah's reformation establishes him as the ideal king. Yet even as the writer celebrates Josiah's pious acts, the voice of YHWH warns that this reformation will not, ultimately, save Judah (22:20; 23:26-27). After the surprising assassination of the king beloved to YHWH, the course of events moves quickly to demonstrate the truth of that warning. The last four kings of Judah struggle under the baneful hegemony first of Egypt and then of Babylon, suffering vassalage, imprisonment, torture, and exile. Finally, the saga culminates in Babylon's siege and conquest of Jerusalem.

These twilight years of Judah, a small kingdom trapped between neighbors overgreedy for hegemony, are represented in the text as two rather parallel sequences of events of equal duration, the first under Egyptian and the second under Babylonian domination. However the actual historical picture may differ from this representation, our text conveys by this sequencing the divine hand at work even in the chaos of destruction. The parallelism of structure may be diagrammed as follows:

I 23:31–24:6 Under Egyptian domination: the reigns of
Jehoahaz and Jehoiakim
A 23:31-35 Jehoahaz
1 Jehoahaz reigns three months (23:31)
2 Jehoahaz imprisoned by Pharaoh Neco who collects tribute from the land (23:33)
3 Pharaoh Neco replaces Jehoahaz with Eliakim, gives him crown name of Jehoiakim (23:34)

4   Pharaoh Neco takes Jehoahaz to Egypt where he dies
(23:35)
B   23:36–24:6 Jehoiakim
5   Jehoiakim reigns eleven years (23:36)
6   Jehoiakim rebels against the king of Babylon (24:1)
7   Attacks on Judah represent YHWH's wrath (24:2-4)
24:7 Transition: King of Egypt retreats under pressure of King of Babylon
I'   24:8–25:7 Under Babylonian domination: the reigns of
Jehoiakin and Zedekiah
A' 24:8-17 Jehoiakin
1'   Jehoiakin reigns three months (24:8)
2'   Jehoiakin taken captive by king of Babylon who takes
Temple and palace treasures (24:12-13)
3'   King Nebuchadnezzar replaces Jehoiakin with
Mattaniah, gives him crown name of Zedekiah (24:17)
4'   King Nebuchadnezzar takes Jehoiakin to Babylon
(24:15)
B' 24:18–25:7 Zedekiah
5'   Zedekiah reigns eleven years (24:18)
6'   Zedekiah rebels against the king of Babylon (25:1)
7'   YHWH rejects Jerusalem and Judah (24:20)

Several motifs associated with Jehoahaz are repeated with Jehoiakin;
similarly a few associated with Jehoiakim recur with Zedekiah. At the
same time, the second pair is not simply a mirror of the first. The king
of Babylon makes his first appearance already during the reign of Jehoiakim, for instance, and the siege of Jerusalem and the exile of various groups is developed only during the reigns of the second pair. Still,
the correspondence of a number of significant details suggests pur-
poseful arrangement by the writer.

Jehoahaz (23:31-35)

Pharaoh Neco, who makes a brief appearance at the end of Josiah's
reign and, in fact, brings it to an end, is the main actor in the account of
the brief three-month tenure of his son Jehoahaz. A perfunctory negative
evaluation of his reign (23:32) is followed by a report of his imprisonment in the north Lebanon valley by Neco, implying a causal link. The
murder of Josiah and imprisonment of Jehoahaz express the suzerainty
of Neco over Judah and areas to the north. Similarly Neco's levying of

heavy tribute (v. 33) and his appointment of Jehoahaz's brother to replace him as king (v. 34) testify to Egypt's domination of Judah. Interestingly, the writer characterizes Neco's placing of Eliakim on the throne as a substitution not for Jehoahaz but for his father Josiah as if the former's brief reign simply did not count. Yet the name change that Neco imposes assigns to Eliakim the theophoric *yĕhô* from the deposed Jehoahaz (*Yĕhôāhāz*). No sooner is Jehoiakim in place than the writer reports the exile of Jehoahaz to Egypt and his death there, precluding a standard formulaic conclusion to the reign of the short-lived king. Instead, before Jehoiakim's reign is formally introduced, the new king is described as raising the silver and gold tribute to satisfy Pharaoh's demand on his predecessor. He turns to the *ʿam hāʾāreṣ* ("people of the land"), the group, we now remember (v. 30), who put Jehoahaz on the throne. That they are the ones now assessed for the indemnity implies that their anointing of Jehoahaz in the wake of Neco's murder of Josiah constituted a challenge to the Pharaoh's authority for which they now must be made to pay.

Jehoiakim (23:36–24:7)

Having finished the report of Jehoiakim's collection of the tribute, imposed as his brother was being carted off to prison, the narrator turns back to give his reign a formal introduction, a carbon copy of that of Jehoahaz. Just as Pharaoh Neco's appearance dominated the account of Jehoahaz, now Nebuchadnezzar's takes over that of Jehoiakim. The announcement of the new invasion ("And in his days King Nebuchadnezzar arose," 24:1) is an exact verbal parallel to the report of Pharaoh Neco's march at the end of Josiah's reign (23:29). The parallel phrasing underscores the double threat confronting Judah, first from the west and now from the east. But the writer is not interested, given Egyptian suzerainty over Judah, in the military confrontation between Babylon and Egypt. Instead he reports simply the capitulation and then, three years later, the rebellion of Jehoiakim against Nebuchadnezzar. What support or lack thereof Jehoiakim received from his former Egyptian overlord is unstated. The focus here is on the theological, not the political.

Against Jehoiakim's rebellion the writer places not Nebuchadnezzar's army but YHWH (although LXX omits "YHWH" implying that Nebuchadnezzar is the subject). Not the regular Babylonian army, but "marauding bands (*gĕdûdim*)" of various ethnicities are bestirred by YHWH to attack and destroy Judah. The effect is to make YHWH into an ally of Babylon against his own people. Indeed, the repetitive theological peroration (vv. 2b-4) cites the warnings of the prophets and the sins of Manasseh, especially his shedding of innocent blood as justification for YHWH's intervention and lack of forgiveness.

Despite the impression of total chaos during Jehoiakim's reign, he is the only one of the last four kings of Judah not to be murdered or exiled and to be accorded a standard regnal conclusion (24:5-6). Following this conclusion and before his successor's file is formally opened, the narrator marks the transition from Egyptian to Babylonian suzerainty (v. 7). Babylon's massive conquest, from the Nile to the Euphrates, also explains, belatedly, why Jehoiakim is depicted as facing Nebuchadnezzar alone without Egyptian help. This transition serves a structural purpose as well, dividing the first two kings from the last two.

Jehoiakin (24:8-17)

The account of the reign of Jehoiakin, only three months long and ending in the young king's imprisonment and exile, parallels in duration and consequence that of his uncle Jehoahaz. As Pharaoh Neco cut short Jehoahaz's reign, so King Nebuchadnezzar nips Jehoiakin's rule as the climax of his siege of the city. As the deposed Jehoahaz is taken to Egypt, the deposed Jehoiakin, along with the entire royal family and various other classes of people, is deported to Babylon. The parallel structure suggests that the Egyptian interlude is a kind of foreshadowing of the final end of Judah. The doubling of the motifs points to divine control even though in both accounts mention of direct divine intervention is absent.

The report of this first exile to Babylon lacks all passion or tension. Considering that Nebuchadnezzar's siege, conquest, and deportation mark the culminating event in the death throes of the kingdom, one might expect great drama. Instead the story is told as though there were a certain inevitability to it. After the formulaic statement of Jehoiakin's misdeeds (24:9), the text records without fanfare that "at that time" the troops of Nebuchadnezzar and then the king himself advance against Jerusalem. As if in a silent, slow motion film, the appearance of Nebuchadnezzar seems to draw forth the surrender of Jehoiakin without the transmission of messages between them. Despite the lack of commentary, the scene of the boy-king surrendering with his mother standing beside him and other royal officials nearby conveys a quiet pathos (v. 12). Pointedly the narrator, who hardly ever dates an event by the regnal years of a foreign ruler, here dates the surrender to the eighth year of Nebuchadnezzar's reign. Because Jehoiakin's reign is over and no successor is yet named, the narrator thereby suggests that the chronological benchmark has passed from Judah to Babylon.

After relating the deposing of the king, the writer goes into greater detail about the looting of the royal treasures and the exiling of Jerusalemites. Verbally echoing the surrender ("and Jehoiakin went out [*wayyēṣēʾ*]," v. 12), the report of the looting ("and he brought out [*wayyôṣēʾ*]," v. 13) of the temple and palace reminds one of earlier raids on the same structures. Indeed gold decorations from the sanctuary (*hēkal*) had earlier been offered to the king of Assyria by Hezekiah. These, though, are attributed to Solomon himself to underscore the significance of the treasures being taken. After the treasures are brought out, the people are taken into exile, listed by category and, in some cases, enumerated. In the midst of the list Jehoiakin is mentioned by name, and his destination, Babylon, is now specified. The totality of the exile is emphasized by the repeated use of "all" and by the final note that only the poorest of the people of the land were left.

The account of the reign of Jehoiakin does not end with his death. The lack of closure opens up a gap about his fate in Babylon. In fact, as we soon see, he is heard about again. But as in the case of his uncle Jehoahaz, deposed by the Egyptians, now Jehoiakin, deposed by the Babylonians, is replaced by another uncle, Mattaniah. His name too is changed, perhaps as an act of loyalty to his Babylonian patron. Zedekiah's reign begins, then, on the heels of the unclosed but clearly ended reign of Jehoiakin.

Zedekiah (24:18–25:7)

Although he has just reported that Zedekiah's immediate predecessor, his court, his army, and his skilled tradesmen went into exile in Babylon—clearly a catastrophe of the first magnitude—the writer opens the account of Zedekiah's reign with the standard regnal formula, attributing to him the same formulaic evil deeds. In this attribution, however, Zedekiah is compared specifically to Jehoiakim, his brother, rather than to his ancestors in general. This comparison directs our attention to the equivalent eleven year reigns of the two kings and to the parallel course of their kingships. It is no little irony that the name given to the last king of Judah by the king of Babylon means "the righteousness of YHWH," for it is that righteous anger, we are reminded (24:20), that spells the end for the nation. This theological headline, though understated, casts its shadow over the horrific events immediately to be narrated. Though divine agency is not directly attributed to Babylon's actions, the parallel with the somewhat more extensive theological commentary in 24:2b-4 makes the point quite clear.

Joined to this verse announcing YHWH's "throwing off" of Jerusalem and Judah is the notice that "Zedekiah rebelled against the king of Babylon" (v. 20b). We are given neither the date nor the motivation for the rebellion, though its paratactic link with YHWH's vengeance indicates that its importance is only as the catalyst for that vengeance. What the writer describes is not the revolt but the Babylonian reaction: the siege of the city and capture of the king. Now precise dates are given, of the beginning (25:1) and end (v. 3) of a siege lasting about a year and a half. Specifying the exact day of the regnal year of Zedekiah that Nebuchadnezzar moves against Jerusalem (v. 1), the writer employs a rare biblical word *(dayeq)* to denote a particular element of the siege building (wall? tower?) that the Babylonians constructed all around the city. From this description of the outside of the city, the writer turns to the inside, noting the effects of the famine (v. 2).

Staying with the inside perspective, the writer records that the breach of the city wall occurs at the depths of the famine: "the city was broken into" (v. 4). Next we hear of the escape of the king and soldiers (the verb has dropped out of the Hebrew, suggesting in its absence the stealth and speed of the escape) through a specified gate and toward the Arabah (the wilderness south of the Dead Sea) eluding the Chaldeans surrounding the city. No voices interrupt the flight or the consequent pursuit by the Chaldeans. Instead the hopelessness of the Judean army is conveyed by the information that Zedekiah was deserted by his troops and left to be captured alone (v. 5).

Logistically the end of Zedekiah's reign bears an unhappy symmetry to that of Jehoahaz, the first of the last four kings of Judah. Like him, Zedekiah, when captured, is taken to Riblah, once Pharaoh Neco's administrative center and now Nebuchadnezzar's, and then taken off into exile, not to Egypt, however, but to Babylon. The object of all but one verb in the last two verses about him, Zedekiah's end is especially gruesome. Brought before Nebuchadnezzar directly, he is arraigned (literally "and they spoke the law to him," [v. 6]) and summarily punished. Repeating for maximum effect the word "eyes" and leading off with the victims as direct objects, the writer has Zedekiah's sons slaughtered "before his eyes" and then Zedekiah's own "eyes" blinded (v. 7). If the murder of Zedekiah's sons is his last vision, our last vision of him is his being led to Babylon by his captors. No formulaic conclusion wraps up the reign of this last king.

Chapter 31

THE AFTERMATH IN JERUSALEM, JUDAH, AND BABYLON

2 Kings 25:8-30

The end of Jerusalem (25:8-21)

With the king—the king appointed by Nebuchadnezzar—blinded and deported, the narrative turns back to what remains in Jerusalem: the buildings and the people not taken into exile. The arrival of Nebuzaradan, a high officer of Nebuchadnezzar, is dated not according to the reign of Zedekiah, which is now over, but rather according to that of the Babylonian king. Babylonian time is thus imposed on Jerusalem even before the final plundering begins. Nebuzaradan is termed *rab-tabbāḥîm* ("chief cook"), apparently a Hebrew translation of the actual Akkadian title by which he is known in Babylonian records. The Hebrew word carries with it as well the connotation "executioner," a fitting description of the person about to wreak destruction upon the city.

First he attacks the buildings, burning, in descending order of importance, temple, palace, and "all the houses of Jerusalem" (v. 9). A concluding clause clarifies, "and all the large houses he burned with fire." After the houses are burned, the Chaldean forces tear down the walls of the city, and after the walls Nebuzaradan goes after the people, leaving only the poorest to keep a modicum of agricultural life alive. The completeness of the exile is underscored by including even those who sided with the Babylonians.

Against this picture of destruction the writer next sets the holy objects of the temple that survived and were taken as booty back to Babylon. The objects are listed as an inventory of plundered sancta, a verbal witness to what was and is, for the author, no more. First the

169

bronze (vv. 13-14) and then the silver and gold (v. 15) objects are listed. Verses 16-17 lavish particular attention on the bronze columns, boasting about the weight of the bronze and the size and decoration of the capitals. This description seeks to capture the glory of the temple metonymically, a last view of the holy objects and the columns that once supported the holy place before they are gone forever. Patiently, the text lists the Temple vessels despoiled in the same order in which they were manufactured (1 Kings 7).[6]

Finally Nebuzaradan takes revenge on notables in the Zedekian administration and on commoners as well. The strategy seems to be to take representatives from a number of groups as examples to the others. The responsibilities of several of the officers are specified as if to memorialize professions destroyed along with the kingship and the state. After listing the chief and deputy priests by name and other royal and military functionaries by office, the narrator records their trek to Nebuchadnezzar at Riblah, where Zedekiah was taken, and their swift executions. Rather than simply stating that they were killed, the narrator collects them all before us, brings them to the king, and only then, without warning, announces their deaths. The last clause of v. 21, "and Judah was exiled from off of its land" recalls the specification of divine causation for the exile in 24:20 that introduces the account of Zedekiah and rounds off the account. The placement of this conclusion thus interprets the executions of the officers and commoners as the official end of the life of Judah on its land. Striking is the lack of theological editorializing such as that interpreting the fall of the North in 2 Kings 17. After all of the prophetic warnings and reminders of those warnings, the fall of Judah is reported in a factual style without any stress on YHWH's judgment, vengeance, or justice. Perhaps the text is all the more powerful for its restraint. Perhaps Judah's end is just too sad for further comment.

Gedaliah's ill-fated regime at Mizpah (25:22-26)

Although v. 21 would seem to offer a definitive conclusion to the story of the kingdom of Judah—"thus Judah was exiled from its land"—one more short section, coda-like, returns to the theme of those who remain. Beginning with a subordinate clause, the narrator identifies the

---

[6] George Savran, "1 and 2 Kings," *The Literary Guide to the Bible,* ed. Robert Alter and Frank Kermode (Cambridge: Harvard, 1987) 148.

people before explaining their fate: "As for the people who remained in the land of Judah, whom the king of Babylon left there, he put in charge of them Gedaliah, son of Ahikam, son of Shaphan." As the grandson of Shaphan, King Josiah's scribe who returned from the mission to the high priest Hilkiah with the all-important scroll, and the son of Ahikam, who along with Shaphan approached the prophet Huldah on behalf of Josiah, Gedaliah comes with a loyalist and bureaucratic pedigree that makes him a logical choice as administrator for the Babylonian authority. The brief account of Gedaliah's regime, however, exists not to explain his administration but rather the rebellion against it. Thus no sooner is he named than he receives a delegation of four named army officers accompanied, we are twice ominously reminded, by "their men" (v. 23) apparently challenging his authority. What they said to him we are not told, but Gedaliah seems eager to pacify them. Have they challenged his rule, threatened to kill him if he is not loyal to them? Clearly they, the military brass, have been passed over in favor of a royalist functionary. After swearing an oath, perhaps promising that they would not be punished by the Babylonian victor, Gedaliah seeks to calm their fears and secure their loyalty to the king of Babylon. Indeed, as the only quoted direct address in chaps. 24–25, Gedaliah's words thematize, perhaps, the writer's final view (the latter part of which seems borne out by the subsequent report about Jehoiakin): "Remain in the land and serve the king of Babylon so that it will go well for you" (v. 24). They have come to Gedaliah in Mizpah, a provincial town identified with Tell-en-Nasbeh about eight miles north of Jerusalem, apparently not destroyed by the Babylonians, where his administration is located.

The gap opened by the silence of the military delegation is filled when, on the heel of Gedaliah's pacific words, one member of the delegation strikes him dead. Beginning with a consequential *wayĕhî* ("and so it was that"), v. 25 reports the assassination of Gedaliah by Ishmael whose name, like that of his victim, here includes two generations of lineage. Now we are also told that he is "of royal seed," a motivation for his capital opposition to both Babylonian rule and the Judean puppet now administering it. The length of Gedaliah's rule is not given, only the vague date of "the seventh month" for his assassination by Ishmael and his ten-man hit squad. That they killed, in addition, the Judeans and Chaldeans supporting Gedaliah indicates that the attack was not merely a personal vendetta but rather a revolt against Babylonian rule. That is further indicated by the report of the flight of everyone left in Judah, the inclusiveness of the exodus (historical data notwithstanding) indicated by the phrase describing those who fled as including "from young to old," to Egypt. The narrator supplies their motivation: fear of the Chaldeans.

An expanded version of Gedaliah's ill-fated regime is found in Jeremiah 40–41. All of the information, indeed the very language, of our passage is found there, but the presence of several topics not found in 2 Kgs 25:22-26 gives the whole a different slant. In particular, Jeremiah includes a longer speech by Gedaliah encouraging inhabitants to settle down in Judean towns, a dialogue about Ishmael's conspiracy against Gedaliah, a story about Ishmael's plots against and killing of Judeans loyal to Gedaliah, and an account of the pursuit of Ishmael by Yohanan, son of Kareah, one of those who had, with Ishmael, approached Gedaliah at the beginning of the story. Whether the version in Kings is a digest of Jeremiah or Jeremiah is a midrash on Kings, the clipped narrative of Kings clearly functions in its context primarily to explain how the remnant in Judah wound up in Egypt, despite the leadership of Gedaliah.

Meanwhile back in Babylon (25:27-30)

Abruptly and surprisingly the scene shifts from the refugees fleeing to Egypt from the Babylonians to King Jehoiakin in exile in Babylon. The writer has never taken us to Babylon before, but now with the temple destroyed, Jerusalem a ghost town, leadership executed, and Judeans scattered, the only continuity with the past is the last living king. Compared to the account of the brutality and totality of the Babylonian revenge on Zedekiah and his court, the earlier description of the exile of Jehoiakin and his court appears quite civilized. The exile of Jehoiakin opened a gap which only now, after the story of Judah has reached its dreadful end, does the writer fill in by making us recall that we do not know what became of the deported king.

True to his regnal framework, the writer introduces his brief glimpse of Jehoiakin in Babylon by dating the event—not, however, by the year of his reign, but by the year of his exile. By employing, even after the destruction, the same dating scheme that had organized his history heretofore, the writer imposes a comforting order on the chaos of an exile stretching into the future. Furthermore, the date specified to the exact day from the time of Jehoiakin's exile is the date of the accession of the new Babylonian king, Evil-Merodach, who is thereby subordinated in some sense to the "reigning" Jehoiakin, consistently called "king of Judah" here. And it is on that very day of his succession that Evil-Merodach releases Jehoiakin from prison. Clearly the report of the simultaneity of the accession and the release is meant not only to bode well for Jehoiakin but also to suggest the divine hand protecting the scion of David.

The images of release here also connote good fortune. The phrase "lifted up the head," for instance, echoes the fate of the chief cupbearer in the Joseph story released from prison by Pharaoh (Gen 40:13) and restored to his former office. In fact, Joseph changed his clothes before appearing before Pharaoh (Gen 41:14) and being elevated to second-in-command just as Jehoiakin does here before he is given a throne which is placed above those of other exiled royalty. An even closer parallel is the account of the high priest Joshua in Zech 3:1-7 who is ordered by the angel of YHWH to take off his filthy garments and put on new ones in preparation for his return to office after surviving exile in Babylonia. In addition to giving Jehoiakin new garments, Evil-Merodach "spoke with him good words," an expression that in cognate languages signifies the making of a treaty.[7] Here the phrase suggests that by showing favor to Jehoiakin, the Babylonian king would have hoped to retain the loyalty of the exiles. Finally, the special food provisions offered to Jehoiakin "all the days of his life" (v. 30) point ever so subtly to hope for the future beyond the destruction.

---

[7] Jon D. Levenson, "The Last Four Verses of Kings," *Journal of Biblical Literature* 103 (1984) 356.

SUGGESTIONS FOR FURTHER READING

As a book that chronicles the reigns of the kings of Israel and Judah, 2 Kings as a whole has tended to attract historical, rather than literary, commentary. The aims of my work are, therefore, not fully realized in the commentaries upon which I relied, although I am indebted to them for many of the ideas developed here. The following commentaries, in particular, proved most valuable:

Cogan, Mordecai and Hayim Tadmor. *II Kings*. The Anchor Bible. Doubleday and Company, Inc., 1988. This is the best and most recent of the historical commentaries.

Hobbs, T.R. *2 Kings*. Word Biblical Commentary. Waco: Word Books, 1985. Having an explicitly theological aim, this commentary also offers keen observations about form, structure, and setting.

Long, Burke O. *2 Kings*. The Forms of the Old Testament Literature 10. Ed. Rolf P. Knierim and Gene M. Tucker. Grand Rapids: William B. Eerdmans, 1991. In addition to its form-critical concerns, this commentary is deeply literary and includes voluminous bibliographical information.

Savran, George. "1 and 2 Kings," *The Literary Guide to the Bible*. Ed. Robert Alter and Frank Kermode, 146–64. Cambridge: Harvard University Press, 1987. Not a commentary but a thoughtful essay about the structure and themes of Kings.

In addition to these general commentaries, some studies of particular narratives in 2 Kings proved to be especially helpful.

Barre, Lloyd M. *The Rhetoric of Political Persuasion: The Narrative Artistry and Political Intentions of 2 Kings 9–11*. The Catholic Biblical Quarterly Monograph Series 20. Washington, DC: The Catholic Biblical Association of America, 1988.

Fewell, Danna N. "Sennacherib's Defeat: Words at War in 2 Kings 18:13–19:37." *Journal for the Study of the Old Testament* 34 (1986) 79–90.

Garcia-Treto, Francisco O. "The Fall of the House: A Carnivalesque Reading of 2 Kings 9 and 10." *Journal for the Study of the Old Testament* 46 (1990) 47–65.

Knoppers, Gary N. "There Was None Like Him: Incomparability in the Books of Kings." *Catholic Biblical Quarterly* 54 (1992) 411–31.

Knoppers, Gary N. *Two Nations Under God: The Deuteronomistic History of Solomon and the Dual Monarchies.* Vol. 2: *The Reign of Jeroboam, the Fall of Israel, and the Reign of Josiah.* Harvard Semitic Monographs 53. Atlanta: Scholars Press, 1994.

Levenson, Jon D. "The Last Four Verses in Kings." *Journal of Biblical Literature* 103 (1984) 353–61.

Mullen, E. Theodore. "The Royal Dynastic Grant to Jehu and the Structure of the Book of Kings." *Journal of Biblical Literature* 107 (1988) 193–206.

Rofé, Alexander. *The Prophetical Stories.* Jerusalem: The Magnes Press, 1988.

Sternberg, Meir. "Time and Space in Biblical (Hi)story Telling: The Grand Chronology." *The Book and the Text: The Bible and Literary Theory,* ed. Regina Schwartz, 81–145. London: Blackwell, 1990.

Viviano, Pauline A. "2 Kings 17: A Rhetorical and Form-Critical Analysis." *Catholic Biblical Quarterly* 49 (1987) 548–59.

The most important, difficult, and, in some ways, controversial work that aims to interpret the literary system operative in biblical narrative is:

Sternberg, Meir. *The Poetics of Biblical Narrative: Ideological Literature and the Drama of Reading.* Bloomington: Indiana University Press, 1985.

GENERAL INDEX

INDEX OF SCRIPTURAL REFERENCES